John Dewey and the Future of Community College Education

ALSO AVAILABLE FROM BLOOMSBURY

14-18 - A New Vision for Secondary Education, Kenneth Baker
John Dewey, Richard Pring
Class and the College Classroom, edited by Robert C. Rosen

FORTHCOMING

Readings for Reflective Teaching in Further, Adult and Vocational Education, edited by Margaret Gregson, Andrew Pollard, Lawrence Nixon and Trish Spedding
Reflective Teaching in Further, Adult and Vocational Education, Margaret Gregson and Yvonne Hillier
Reflective Teaching in Higher Education, Paul Ashwin

John Dewey and the Future of Community College Education

CLIFFORD P. HARBOUR

Bloomsbury Academic
An imprint of Bloomsbury Publishing Plc

B L O O M S B U R Y
LONDON · NEW DELHI · NEW YORK · SYDNEY

Bloomsbury Academic

An imprint of Bloomsbury Publishing Plc

50 Bedford Square	1385 Broadway
London	New York
WC1B 3DP	NY 10018
UK	USA

www.bloomsbury.com

BLOOMSBURY and the Diana logo are trademarks of Bloomsbury Publishing Plc

First published 2015

© Clifford P. Harbour, 2015

British Library Cataloguing-in-Publication Data
A catalogue record for this book is available from the British Library.

ISBN: HB: 978-1-4411-2275-9
PB: 978-1-4411-7292-1
ePub: 978-1-4411-7506-9
ePDF: 978-1-4411-2609-2

Library of Congress Cataloging-in-Publication Data
A catalog record for this book is available from the Library of Congress.

Typeset by Deanta Global Publishing Services, Chennai, India
Printed and bound in the United States of America

Contents

Preface vi

Introduction 1

PART ONE   The context 15

1 The contemporary community college 17
2 The community college of the future 32
3 Introducing John Dewey 44

PART TWO   The evolution of the community college 57

4 The Junior college movement 59
5 The Great Depression and the junior college 74
6 The late twentieth century normative vision 87
7 Turning to a new normative vision 100

PART THREE   Dewey on education, democracy,
                  and community 115

8 The relationship between democracy and education 117
9 The Great Society and the Great Community 127
10 Dewey and the Great Depression 141
11 The Deweyan community college 152

Bibliography 161
Index 175

Preface

Over the last 50 years, the community college has improved the lives of millions of Americans by offering an inexpensive and convenient pathway to good jobs and university study. Its long record of institutional growth and increasing enrollments has created an appearance of stability and permanence. But, now, in an era of austerity, the community college commitment to open access, the centerpiece of its traditional mission, is being challenged. Policymakers, legislators, and private foundations are calling upon community colleges to retain their commitment to access while also significantly improving their graduation rates. Privately, community college presidents admit that when their institutions are asked to emphasize completion, they must reallocate resources and compromise access.

What should community colleges do? Embrace a new mission of access *and* completion? Surrender their traditional commitment to access and emphasize credential completion? Should they stand firm and reject the new call for completion? This debate reveals a problem that has plagued community colleges and their institutional predecessors, the junior colleges, for more than a century. In a hierarchical, status-driven, and heavily subsidized industry, community colleges have been forced to prioritize the interests of institutional outsiders over the needs of their students. This problem will not be corrected overnight. But, if community colleges are to gain greater autonomy and better prepare their students for the future, they will need a new vision of what they might be in the decades ahead. I propose that they adopt a vision that prioritizes individual growth and the development of democratic communities. John Dewey, the American philosopher and educator, articulated such a vision 100 years ago. But the pieces of this vision were spread over 30 years of books, articles, and speeches. In this work, I revisit Dewey's writings, describe the life experiences that helped shape them, and pull together the key points that might serve as the foundation for a new community college normative vision. This book explains, therefore, what John Dewey can do for the community college of the future.

This project is the outcome of conversations with community college students, university graduate students, community college faculty and staff, community college presidents, university professors, and policymakers.

Many had a hand in influencing the direction of this book. They include former colleagues at Durham Technical Community College, Bill Ingram and Phail Wynn. My former professors at North Carolina State University and Duke University provided a foundation for the interpretation unpacked below and they were George Vaughan, George Baker, and Rick Roderick. Education faculty at Colorado State University and the University of Wyoming also offered insights about community colleges and John Dewey and these associates were Timothy Gray Davies, Bill Timpson, and Michael Day. David Hardy, Gert Biesta, Jennifer Wolgemuth, Ozan Jaquette, John Levin, Sue Kater, and Doug Smith are researchers and scholars at other institutions who have provided me with advice and inspiration. My former doctoral students, many of whom have now gone on to senior leadership positions at community colleges, also had a great influence on this project. Of course, none of these people is responsible for my errors.

This essay begins a conversation and passes it along to my principal audience—community college students, faculty, staff, and administrators. I invite them to consider how their college might use the work of John Dewey to truly become "Democracy's College." The book is dedicated to Suzanne who attended Casper College and later, as a researcher and educator, never lost sight of this simple fact: at its core, higher education should be about the students. They are the future.

Note on sources

The source for John Dewey's books, articles, and speeches is the 38-volume *Collected Works of John Dewey* edited by Jo Ann Boydston and published by the Southern Illinois University Press (2008 edition). The source for John Dewey's correspondence is *The Correspondence of John Dewey, 1871–1952 (I–IV)*, Electronic Edition, edited by Larry Hickman and published by the InteLex Corporation.

Introduction

The President goes to Macomb Community College

On July 14, 2009, President Barack Obama visited Macomb Community College in Warren, Michigan. It was President Obama's first trip to Michigan after his inauguration in January 2009. An enthusiastic crowd greeted him as he rolled up his shirtsleeves and stepped up to the podium under a sunny blue sky. After acknowledging state and local officials, the President reminded his audience that he was working hard to secure federal support for the ailing automobile industry. He assured them that he was well aware of their struggles, living in a state that had been hit very hard by the ongoing recession.

However, the main purpose of his visit was to introduce his American Graduation Initiative (Obama's speech at Macomb Community College, July 14, 2009). The American Graduation Initiative (AGI) was the President's plan to significantly increase the number of students graduating from American colleges and universities. At Macomb, the President called upon the nation's community colleges to produce an additional 5 million certificate and degree recipients by 2020. To support this college completion initiative, the President proposed a $12 billion federal funding package. The President's proposal to provide new federal funding for community colleges, in particular, was not surprising. During the presidential campaign of 2007–08, the young senator from Illinois repeatedly identified the nation's community colleges, and their mission of expanding educational opportunity, as a vital resource for the nation.

The day after President Obama visited Macomb, Congressman George Miller (Democrat—California) introduced a bill in the United States House of Representatives incorporating the President's educational priorities, including the AGI. This bill, the Student Aid and Fiscal Responsibility Act of 2009, proposed an overhaul of the federal student loan program. It also included plans to appropriate $12 billion, over a period of 10 years, to help community colleges graduate more students. On July 15, *The Washington Post* ran a story on the AGI and included a statement from George Boggs, President of the American Association of Community Colleges (AACC). Boggs said the $12 billion, if approved, would be "the largest federal investment in community college history" (Shear and de Vise, *The Washington Post*, July 15, 2009, p. A2).

President Obama's bold new plan carried the potential to affect the lives of millions of college students. In 2009, community colleges enrolled more than 7.2 million students, approximately 40 percent of all undergraduates (Knapp, Kelly-Reid and Ginder 2011). And, they enrolled a larger share of low-income and underrepresented minority students than public 4-year institutions. But the President's AGI was soon overshadowed by another bold new plan and that was his national health care initiative, the Patient Protection and Affordable Care Act, or as it became known, "Obamacare."

The priorities of the federal government

The new President's domestic policy agenda was ambitious and it soon became clear that his health care initiative was the top priority. In March 2010, in a final rush of legislative activity, Congress passed Obamacare along with revisions to the federal student loan program. Also included in the legislation was $2 billion for the Department of Labor to pay community colleges for training dislocated workers. However, the $12 billion promised as part of the AGI at Macomb and initially included in the Student Aid and Fiscal Responsibility Act, was left out.

Over the next year, the Obama administration continued to spotlight community colleges as a vital component of the American higher education system. In October 2010, the President hosted a White House summit on community colleges, attended by community college leaders from across the nation. But the President's first 2 years in office were a disappointment for community colleges. He continued to call upon these institutions to significantly increase their graduation rates. But he could not deliver the resources he believed were needed to get the job done (Marcus July 11, 2011).

In November 2010, the Democrats lost control of the House of Representatives and political gridlock halted progress on most domestic policy initiatives. Two years later, in November 2012, President Obama was reelected but prospects for greater funding for community colleges (and most other domestic policy priorities) were overshadowed by four serious problems that confronted the federal government and hobbled the nation. First, the political climate in Washington D.C. was highly polarized and this prevented the development of problem solving alliances that crossed party lines. For example, the Republican hardliners in the House of Representatives tried to block the implementation of Obamacare, the President's signature legislative accomplishment, even after a conservative United States Supreme Court had upheld its constitutionality in June 2012. Second, the slow recovery from the Financial Crisis of 2007–08 and the Great Recession of 2007–09, led to an extended period of unusually low economic growth and high unemployment. Before the Financial Crisis began, in January 2007, national unemployment was 4.6 percent. But it rose for the next 2 and 1/2 years until it peaked at 10 percent in October 2009. It remained above 7 percent until December 2013. One consequence of these two economic problems was that state and federal governments were spending more on relief programs, taking in less in the form of tax receipts, and laying off their own public employees. Third, by 2012, the nation's War against Terror was entering a second decade. For 10 years the battle had been fought in Iraq, Afghanistan, Yemen, Somalia, and Pakistan. In the summer of 2013, however, Americans learned that their e-mail and telephone communications were being secretly tracked by American security services in an effort to get ahead of the terrorists (Scahill 2013). The cost of the war to Americans had been substantial: 5,000 combat deaths, 50,000 wounded, a war debt estimated at $6 trillion, and the loss of privacy. Finally, the federal government's bailout of banks and major industries during the Financial Crisis exacerbated an already difficult budget situation. When combined with Washington's longstanding inability to manage and fund entitlements, the federal government's debt ballooned from $9 trillion in September 2007 to $17 trillion in November 2013 (United States Treasury Department, TreasuryDirect, Monthly Statement of the Public Debt of the United States, November 30, 2013).

These problems effectively neutralized efforts to address many domestic problems and one of these was the college completion problem. Washington's chronic inability to act, however, did not stop others from moving forward. Back in 2009, leaders from state government, the business community, policy think tanks, and higher education, came together and established Complete College America, a nonprofit organization, dedicated to improving the nation's college completion numbers. Other nonprofits and major philanthropies were soon working alongside Complete College America. Together these groups articulated what has become known as "The Completion Agenda."

The Completion Agenda

The Completion Agenda is best understood as a broad reform movement asserting, as its central claim, that American colleges and universities must produce substantially more graduates over the next 10 years. Two arguments have been offered to justify this claim. First, Completion Agenda advocates argue that the United States needs to produce more college graduates so employers can hire the talent needed to develop, produce, and sell new products and services in the global marketplace. If the nation does not produce these graduates, businesses will not be able to produce these new goods and services and many will lose out to foreign competition. Over the short term, a failure to produce more college graduates will curtail American economic growth and extend high unemployment. Over the long term, however, this failure will lead to national economic decline. Second, they claim that unless American colleges and universities graduate more students, the rise in income inequality, which began in the late 1970s, will continue to grow. The argument here is that students who do not earn a college credential will be unable to secure high-paying jobs. Their inability to significantly increase personal income, when compared to the extended and significant increase in earnings for people in the highest income bracket, means that income inequality will continue to grow. These two economic arguments—both national in scope—are the overriding justification for the Completion Agenda. The Completion Agenda and its supporting arguments are a prime example of the economic logic now framing many public higher education issues.

This logic is based on four broad assumptions that are the cornerstones of neoliberal political philosophy. The first is that in a complex twenty-first-century democracy, market forces (as opposed to government institutions) are the more efficient and effective mechanism to apportion all but the most basic social opportunities, benefits, and risks. Second, government regulation of markets should be limited in order to promote freer trade. The third is that, in general, public debt should be limited in order to reduce tax burdens and facilitate greater private investment. The fourth is that higher education is essentially a private good that should be managed and delivered in such a way to limit public expenditures while promoting students' future financial success. These broad assumptions, although rejected by many social scientists, exercise a strong hold on many state and federal politicians and on much of the American public.

Reclaiming the American Dream

For community colleges, an important chapter in the emergence of the Completion Agenda was written in April 2012. Then, AACC, the nation's largest advocacy organization representing community colleges, released its report: *Reclaiming the American Dream: Community Colleges and the*

Nation's Future (*Reclaiming the American Dream*) (AACC 2012). *Reclaiming the American Dream* advocated a top to bottom transformation of community colleges through the implementation of seven recommendations. The first and most important recommendation also described the primary objective of the transformation, which was to,

> Increase completion rates of students earning community college credentials (certificates and associate degrees) by 50% by 2020, while preserving access, enhancing quality, and eradicating attainment gaps associated with income, race, ethnicity, and gender. (AACC 2012, p. x)

Each of the remaining six recommendations proposed changes to help accomplish this new objective. The overall transformation would involve restructuring of the community college workforce, eliminating high cost/ low enrollment programs, and developing new programs and services to accelerate student progress. *Reclaiming the American Dream* was specific in explaining the need for the transformation. The authors contended that the nation's economy was in crisis and community colleges needed to help resolve it. The report stated,

> In a rapidly changing America and a drastically reshaped world, the ground beneath the nation's feet has shifted so dramatically that community colleges need to reimagine their roles and the ways they do their work. The premise of this . . . [report] can be summarized in three sentences: The American Dream is at risk. Because a highly educated population is fundamental to economic growth and a vibrant democracy, community colleges can help reclaim that dream. But stepping up to this challenge will require dramatic redesign of these institutions, their mission, and, most critically, their students' educational experiences. (AACC 2012, p. vii)

Reclaiming the American Dream repeated the two-part rationale that has guided the Completion Agenda. First, a highly educated population is essential to the nation's economic future. Second, income inequality will continue to grow unless more students graduate from college.

The desire to transform community colleges so they might produce more completers is understandable. As I noted above, community colleges enroll more than 40 percent of all undergraduate students. They also enroll a disproportionate share of underrepresented minorities and low-income students. Improving the college completion rates for these students would be good for the students and the society. However, there is another reason why the Completion Agenda is focused heavily on community colleges. Compared to universities and liberal arts colleges, community colleges have significantly lower graduation rates.

For example, in 2011, Complete College America reported that only 18.8 percent of full-time community college students complete a 2-year associate's degree in 4 years (Complete College America 2011). Only 27.8 percent of full-time community college students complete a 1-year certificate program in 2 years. If Completion Agenda advocates are correct about the positive consequences that will follow from higher graduation rates, community colleges are a great place to concentrate our efforts in addressing the two economic problems motivating the reform movement. Higher completion rates at the community college could benefit the nation's economy and help limit income inequality while focusing on an institution that has room for improvement.

The challenge

And, this is where community colleges are today. They have been assigned a heavy responsibility, to significantly increase graduation rates. But they approach this assignment while retaining their commitment to expand educational opportunity and also while the nation is preoccupied with looming domestic and foreign problems. And they approach the assignment with no new federal money to fund an institutional transformation regarded by many as substantial, necessary, and urgent. To be sure, community college graduation rates must improve. Nobody is suggesting otherwise.

But, as a group, community colleges are especially vulnerable to the political pressure being placed on all higher education institutions to increase graduation rates. They are low-status institutions in an industry obsessed with rankings. They do not enjoy the institutional histories and traditions that usually temper political encroachment on the campuses of liberal arts colleges and universities. Community colleges also lack the powerful alumni willing to advocate for their *alma mater* in state capitols. Finally, as a group of institutions, community colleges rely heavily upon state appropriations and federal financial aid and could suffer greatly if a significant portion of these funds was tied to improved graduation rates. The Completion Agenda represents, therefore, a significant challenge to the future of American community college education. The nature of this challenge needs to be clearly understood. To repeat a point I made earlier, the question is not whether community colleges need to improve their graduation rates. This must be done. But, is a vision advocating access and completion the best we can imagine? In this book, I argue that the students, faculty, staff, and administrators at community colleges should begin the process of creating their own local community-based movements dedicated to identifying problems, developing community solutions, and reinvigorating democracy.

These are not easy times for community colleges but they are not as unique as we might think. As Mark Twain is reported to have said, "History doesn't repeat itself, but it does rhyme." Almost 100 years ago, John Dewey (1859–1952), was completing a book, *Democracy and Education* (published in 1916), that would confirm his reputation as a leading philosopher, educator, and public intellectual. Dewey's purpose in writing the book was to explain the kind of education needed to advance American democracy in a period distinguished by rapid technological change, a powerful but unregulated economy, growing inequality in income and wealth, and great demographic change as a result of immigration. Dewey was committed to expanding access to public education. But he also recognized that in a democracy, educational institutions needed to do more than offer students access and award credentials. Students also needed to understand how they might live and work in a modern democracy. Over the next 25 years Dewey continued to focus on the relationship between democracy and education, something he addressed in books, articles, and speeches. The distinguishing quality of these writings was his optimism that Americans could improve their democracy and thereby create a more just and equitable society. But this progress would not be the consequence of new laws or policies or the creation of new government agencies. Progress would be made because people would change how they interacted with one another and lived in their community.

In the chapters that follow, I argue that today Dewey's works are an excellent source to turn to in order to reacquaint ourselves with the relationship between democracy and education. More specifically, I contend that Dewey's writings and speeches identify and explain the values and priorities that may serve as the building blocks to develop a new normative vision for community colleges. This Deweyan vision acknowledges that community colleges must improve access and completion. But they must do much more than this. In an era when the American political system seems to stumble from one crisis to the next and the economy does not work for most Americans, community colleges must provide their students with the ability and confidence to see how they too might play a role in developing a democracy that works for everyone.

The objectives of the book

Given this context, this book has three major tasks. First, I explain the development of the community college and its institutional predecessor, the junior college, to show how it acquired its traditional vision of expanding educational opportunity. I also explain how and why this traditional vision has become challenged by the Completion Agenda. Second, I provide an introduction to John Dewey and his writings to identify the building blocks for a new normative vision for the American community college. This new vision acknowledges the importance of expanding educational opportunity and promoting completion. But it goes beyond these to articulate commitments to individual growth and the development of democratic communities. Finally, I identify and explain the values and priorities that would comprise a Deweyan normative vision for the community college of the future.

Qualifications

Before moving forward, a few qualifications are in order. First, and most importantly, throughout this book, but especially in the first few chapters, my description of the community college and the junior college places both institutions within the context of American education. This description is not comprehensive. It is not my intent to offer a history of the junior college or the community college. Instead, my goal is to highlight aspects of the junior college movement and the subsequent expansion of community colleges to illuminate the values and priorities that guided the evolution of these institutions. This review reveals that for decades, junior colleges struggled to articulate their educational purposes. Their evolution was, in a word, haphazard. And, during these confusing years, the values and priorities that guided the development of junior colleges were supplied by high schools, universities, parents, religious organizations, and employers. Only with the end of World War II, and the transformation of traditional junior colleges into new community colleges, did the expansion of educational opportunity for adults become the top priority. This vision of expanding educational opportunity became inscribed in federal and state higher education legislation. It also provided the rationale for the funding streams that support community colleges today.

In 2007, however, education policymakers and politicians signaled their intentions to modify this vision when the United States fell into the worst economic crisis since the Great Depression. This crisis led education policymakers and politicians to endorse the Completion Agenda as a strategy that would help the nation recover. Thus, expanding educational opportunity and completion became the top priority for community colleges. Understanding how this new two-part vision became accepted, however, requires revisiting the evolution of junior colleges and community colleges.

Second, in a discussion of higher education institutions, it is important to distinguish institutional mission from normative vision. Briefly stated, for public institutions, a college or university's mission is created by the state legislature and the institution's governing board. Usually, a state legislature will pass a law establishing the general purpose of an institution or class of institutions. This legislation might state, for example, that the institution has the responsibility of conducting research. It might establish the institution's responsibility to serve various industries dominant in the state (e.g., agriculture, engineering, and mining). Finally, state legislation often describes how selective the institution must be in student admissions (e.g., very selective, moderately selective, or open access). With this law in place, institutional governing boards will often clarify their institution's mission by adopting a "mission statement" that incorporates critical language from the state legislation and then supplements this with a focus or purpose consistent with the legislation. A mission statement, therefore, describes an institution's educational role, in general terms, for both the public and people working and studying at the institution. We may defend or criticize an institution's mission. But it is an authoritative statement of what the institution *must* do and is established by law.

A normative vision, on the other hand is different. It is an abstraction, a group of beliefs that, considered together, articulate the ethical purpose or role of an institution or class of institutions. In community college education, normative visions are considered and debated in informal and formal discussions. From time to time, every community college takes up the question, "What should a community college do, in these circumstances?" Usually this topic is discussed informally. People debate this in student government meetings, faculty retreats, at the deans' council, and in the president's leadership team meetings. These conversations are critically important because they are where people come together and share their views about what their college should or should not be doing. This conversation goes beyond what the college *must* do (a matter determined by its mission statement). It examines the aspirations of the college community and discusses what the institution *should* be doing. The limitation of these informal discussions, however, is that usually they are not recorded or shared. Accordingly, they become not just informal but also private and there is no larger public conversation about the values and priorities that should help guide one particular community college or community colleges in general.

The discussion of normative visions also occurs, however, in policy documents and the higher education scholarly literature. When a normative vision is discussed in these texts, it becomes a matter of public record and debate. The formal discussion of a normative vision, therefore, has the advantage of being public and establishing a record for later study. In this book, I rely heavily on works that comprise the formal discussion of the community college normative vision. But my perspective has also been guided by the informal discussion of this topic, something I participated in during my 14 years as a community college instructor and administrator.

Third, although I will rely on Dewey's work to propose a new normative vision for community colleges, I will not offer a philosophical analysis or critique of his arguments. Additionally, in my review of Dewey's work, I focus primarily on his writings concerning education and democracy. A Deweyan normative vision could also be developed in light of his texts on inquiry, communication, logic, and experience. And a Deweyan vision could be developed based on his attention to topics such as science and technology. I leave these other topics and their relevancy to community colleges for others to consider.

Also, throughout the book, I steer clear of the notion that Dewey's writings can supply a normative vision for specific community colleges. Excepting his occasional work as a consultant, Dewey did not give anyone a map explaining how specific communities and institutions might evolve in a more democratic manner. Such a prescriptive approach would be far from "Deweyan" because for him, the reformation of any institution must be grounded in the experience of the individuals at the institution. Dewey's insights only provide us with the conceptual building blocks for developing a new normative vision. The actual work of developing a campus-specific normative vision is the responsibility of specific community college students, faculty, staff, and administrators, working in collaboration with their communities.

Fourth, this book does not offer a critique of the community college. It does not critically examine its curricula, leadership, faculty, or staff. I will not comment directly on instruction, assessment, or student learning. And, this book will not analyze state policies concerning delivery of community college programs and services. In other words, this book does not offer a critique or analysis of practice or policy. Instead, it invites readers to consider the values and priorities that should guide a community college serving students and communities in a democratic society.

Why Dewey?

A new normative vision for community colleges could be constructed using the work of many different theorists. However, John Dewey's work is especially well suited for the task. Dewey was committed to the expansion of educational opportunity. He believed that the quality of our democracy was directly affected by the quality of educational systems. And, he believed that education could provide people with the capacity to come together and collaboratively solve their community problems. Dewey also recognized, however, that life is not fair. He recognized that institutions and policies are created as a result of a political process that is always imperfect. In a democracy, therefore, people needed to be able to regularly reform their institutions in order to make them better. Dewey believed that if people were open-minded, reflective, worked hard, and reached out to one another, they could come together and solve their problems much more effectively than if some external authority dictated the solution. This approach needed to be scientific and experimental and allow for continuing improvement as new information was acquired and analyzed. It also needed to be inclusive and consider the views of all those who might be directly affected by any reform.

Despite Dewey's stature in the academy and his high profile as a public intellectual in the first half of the twentieth century, he has not been a dominant figure in discussions of American higher education. He is rarely mentioned in the community college literature. But Dewey was familiar with the junior college. While a professor at the University of Chicago in the 1890s, he lectured in his institution's new junior college program. Later, some of Dewey's students left their university studies to work at junior colleges. More importantly, Dewey was very concerned about educational opportunity, vocational education, higher education, and democracy—topics that were closely intertwined with the evolution of junior colleges and, later on, community colleges.

Over the last 30 years, the significance of Dewey's contributions on democracy has been affirmed by leading historians and philosophers. Robert Westbrook, a historian, explained that Dewey "crafted a democratic philosophy . . . unparalleled in modern American thought" (Westbrook 1991, p. 552). Sheldon Wolin, a political philosopher, wrote that Dewey had "the dominant voice in political theory during the inter-war years" (Wolin 2004, p. 503). Richard Rorty, another philosopher, summarized the importance of Dewey's insights when he remarked that Dewey would be waiting at the end of the road being traveled by contemporary philosophers working in a variety of Western traditions (Rorty 1982). Dewey's writings often anticipate, sometimes eerily, the issues and problems that challenge us today.

Perhaps more importantly, today, in emerging fields such as science and technology studies, Dewey's philosophy has been used to support new interdisciplinary inquiries examining the relationship between democracy and science (e.g., Brown 2009), the creation of a "public sphere" in technologically advanced democracies (e.g., Rosa 2013), and the ways in which democratic practice is reflected in the material world (e.g., Marres 2013). Dewey's writings, in other words, are not only important as milestones in the history of American thought on democracy and education. They are also shaping the future of democratic thought right now.

The organization of the book

This book is organized in three parts. In Chapters 1, 2, and 3, I set the stage for the discussion that follows and provide some background on the community college and John Dewey for readers who may not be well acquainted with one or the other. In Chapters 4, 5, 6, and 7, I review the events and developments that reflected the values and priorities guiding the evolution of junior colleges and community colleges. In Chapters 8, 9, 10, and 11, I turn to selected works by John Dewey and highlight key issues and themes concerning education and democracy. This discussion identifies the Deweyan values and priorities that may be used to establish a new normative vision for community colleges. I now offer a more detailed introduction for readers desiring a more specific account of individual chapters.

Chapter 1 provides a general introduction to the community college and its role in the American higher education system. I also describe the institution's curriculum, student population, mission, and funding processes. I continue my discussion of the Completion Agenda and focus on its relevancy to community colleges. Then, I review the conventional history of the community college, a history that has become quite popular in the literature and on community college campuses. As I will explain, this history glosses over important developments in the evolution of the institution.

Chapter 2 examines the conditions or drivers that will have a significant influence on higher education in the United States and the community college of the future. These drivers are income inequality, technological change and learning analytics, globalization, generational equity issues, and public higher education funding. For some colleges, the impact of these drivers may be overshadowed by local conditions (e.g., changes in local funding, partnerships with business and area high schools, and significant changes in the local economy). However, generally speaking, the five drivers I discuss are conditions that will affect all institutions to some extent and some institutions to a great extent.

In Chapter 3, I introduce John Dewey. This introduction explains the events that shaped his understanding of the world. It also introduces readers to John Dewey as a figure whose lifespan included the American Civil War (1861–65) and World War II (1939–45). In particular I focus on some of the major historical events that occurred in Chicago and New York while he lived in these cities. I then offer a succinct account of Dewey's view on the role of education in a democracy. I conclude with observations on Dewey's legacy for American education and democracy.

The creation and early evolution of the American junior college, the institutional predecessor to the community college, is addressed in Chapter 4. This period runs from 1900 to 1930. A review of important developments during this period reveals how external interests played a critical role in defining the values and priorities of the junior college. The first junior colleges were created and then expanded to serve the interests of the university and high school. Junior colleges, organized in the first decades of the twentieth century, attempted to secure their place in the American higher education hierarchy by attending to a wide range of institutional problems and needs.

The 1930s was a critical decade in the evolution of junior colleges. I focus on this period in Chapter 5. During this decade, junior colleges continued to expand despite the crippling economic impact of the Great Depression. One of the intriguing developments in this decade was the creation of emergency junior colleges, public 2-year institutions organized primarily by the states but funded by the federal government. I also discuss the adult education movement, a movement that responded to adults' growing desire for education after leaving school. By the end of the 1930s, junior colleges had begun to carve out a future that was more focused on vocational education, a new curriculum that would eventually guarantee their success, and earn the respect of the business community and the state and federal governments.

In Chapter 6, I review the period from 1940 to 1970 and examine events relevant to the continuing development of the junior college and the emergence of the community college. This discussion begins with the United States' entry into World War II and the Servicemen's Readjustment Act of 1944 (the GI Bill of Rights). I then briefly discuss the landmark 1947 report, *Higher Education for American Democracy*, commonly referred to as "the Truman Commission Report" (President's Commission on Higher Education 1947). The Truman Commission Report established a new federal role for higher education and this role has only grown since 1947, with positive and negative consequences for community colleges. I then review the rapid growth of the community college during the 1950s, 1960s, and 1970s. I also examine the special history of community colleges in California, the state that has been the national leader in community college education for most of the last century.

Chapter 7 opens with a review of two critical studies that identified and explained student diversion at community colleges. The student diversion studies published by Clark (in 1960) (Clark 1960a) and Brint and Karabel (in 1989) (Brint and Karabel 1989) were two significant data-based critiques of community colleges. These critiques are noteworthy because they showed that institutions designed to increase educational opportunity also have a less idealistic role in the American higher education hierarchy—specifically, diverting students away from traditional bachelor degree programs. I then examine two important policy documents produced by AACC in 1988 and 2012 that outlined two different normative visions for community colleges. The 1988 text proposed a future where community colleges would serve as the catalyst for community development (AACC 1988). The 2012 report endorsed the Completion Agenda (AACC 2012).

Chapter 8 focuses on Dewey's life as a young professor and *Democracy and Education*, a text he published during World War I that offers his most complete account of the relationship between education and democracy. This book also offers some of Dewey's most important thinking about vocational education and education as a path to social transformation. I also examine Dewey's work in a number of lesser texts that help develop and explain some of the central concepts articulated in *Democracy and Education*.

I continue my focus on Dewey by reviewing selected publications he produced in the 1920s. This discussion is presented in Chapter 9. I begin by highlighting some of Dewey's work that was influenced by World War I. I also provide a brief review of key points from *Human Nature and Conduct*, a text that explained the role of habit in shaping our social dispositions. The chapter's major purpose, however, is to offer observations on *The Public and Its Problems*, Dewey's extended response to Walter Lippmann's devastating critiques of American democracy in the 1920s. In *The Public and Its Problems*, the optimistic Dewey argued that it was not too late for Americans to come together and build a better democracy.

In Chapter 10, I turn to Dewey's work produced in the 1930s. Dewey's writing in these texts offers the most pointed political critiques of his life. These publications show that the problems of education and democracy are intimately connected to the social and economic challenges of the day. By now Dewey was in his 70s and, noting the depth of the Great Depression, warned his readers that Americans needed to be much more intentional in developing a progressive democracy. The rise of totalitarian governments in Germany and the Soviet Union showed that when people are faced with dire economic and social circumstances, they may turn to dictatorships to solve their problems. If Americans did not see a better democracy on the horizon, he feared, they too may consider electing extremists to lead the nation.

In Chapter 11, I revisit key points developed throughout the book and identify, explain, and review the values and priorities that would serve as the basis for a Deweyan normative vision for the twenty-first-century community college. A Deweyan vision for community colleges opens the door for new thinking about how community colleges can play a stronger role in promoting individual growth and developing democratic communities.

PART ONE

The context

1

The contemporary community college

Introduction

Community colleges are a major force in American higher education and the numbers bear this out. In 2013, there were 1,132 community colleges operating in the United States and 986 of these were public, state-funded institutions (AACC, Community College Fact Sheet, 2014). Another 31 colleges were Native American tribal colleges and the remaining 115 were private nonprofit or independent institutions. Community colleges are located in every state in the nation. They operate in the commonwealths of Puerto Rico and the Northern Marina Islands and also in the territories of Guam and American Samoa. California, the largest state in the nation, as measured by population, currently has 114 community colleges in its state community college system. Rhode Island, the smallest state in the union as measured by area, has one community college, with five campuses. Within almost every state, community colleges serve urban, suburban, and rural areas and, accordingly, they vary considerably by size and service area.

In this chapter, I describe contemporary community colleges in general terms. I describe their internal organization and their student population. I also discuss the institution's mission and describe the general parameters for funding these colleges. After completing this introduction, I sharpen our focus on the Completion Agenda and its significance for community colleges in particular. Finally, I outline the conventional history of the community college. This history, like many family histories, overstates the positive and understates the negative. Putting this conventional history on the table, however, will help highlight the importance of other developments which I turn to in Chapters 4, 5, 6, and 7.

The community college—organization and culture

Public community colleges are typically governed by a board of trustees. In some states, board members are elected. In others they are appointed, often by the governor. The board hires the college president and this person is responsible for leading the institution and managing the delivery of all instructional programs and services. The president is also responsible for hiring, developing, promoting, and firing the college's administrators, faculty, and staff. Community college presidents usually hold a terminal degree (usually the Doctor of Education, Ed.D.) and they lead a team of senior administrators who have responsibility for different divisions in the college. Typically, a senior administrator, or vice president, is responsible for one of the following major areas at the college: instructional services (credit programs in the university transfer and occupational program areas), adult and continuing education (noncredit programs in adult and community service areas), student development (admissions, registration, student records, financial aid, and counseling), and administrative services (the business office, human resources, and facilities).

Full-time community college faculty usually have a 5–5 teaching load. This means that they teach 5 three-credit courses each semester. The traditional faculty contract, which covers an academic year, requires full-time teaching for both the fall and spring semesters. This teaching load is usually much heavier than that assigned to full-time faculty at other colleges and universities. At most of these institutions, faculty typically teach 3–2, 2–2, or even 2–1. A substantial majority of the faculty employed by 4-year colleges and universities hold a terminal degree (usually the doctor of philosophy degree, Ph.D.). Most faculty employed by a community college hold a master's degree (master of arts or master of science, M.A. or M.S.) although some only have a bachelor's degree (bachelor of arts or bachelor of science, B.A. or B.S.). Others, especially those teaching in the occupational program areas, sometimes only hold a sub-baccalaureate degree.

Another important difference between community college faculty and faculty teaching at a 4-year college or university is that community college faculty do not have a research and scholarship assignment. Most permanent faculty working at these other institutions must carry out research and scholarship and then publish their findings, although these responsibilities vary greatly from one institution to the next. Still, even a minimal responsibility for research and scholarship usually provides a professor with a greater degree of autonomy in his work. This is because the selection of research and scholarship projects is left to the professor. Community college instructors do not have this responsibility and therefore they also enjoy slightly less independence in their work.

An important consequence of these differences is that the academic culture at a community college tends to be quite different from that found at other colleges and universities. Although there are always exceptions, generally speaking, the culture at a community college tends to focus more intensely on teaching and learning. As a result, the community college campus culture tends to be somewhat less concerned with discipline or field identity. That is, community college faculty will identify as a historian or nurse or accountant. But, they usually identify more strongly with their institution, the community college. Faculty at 4-year colleges and universities, on the other hand, tend to think otherwise. That is, because they conduct at least some research and scholarship in their discipline or field, they usually identify more strongly with their discipline or field than with their institution. This difference in campus culture is one reason why community college instructors tend to be more responsive to institutional change. Their primary loyalty is to the college and not their discipline or field.

The community college student population

There are four important considerations to note when examining college student enrollments and the community college student population. First, student enrollments at community colleges have increased significantly during the last 30 years (1979–2009). But they have remained a relatively constant share of the total undergraduate student population (public and private) (Knapp et al. 2011; Snyder and Dillow 2011). In 1979, the nation's total undergraduate enrollment was just under 10 million and 41 percent of this population or 4 million were community college students. In 2009, American community colleges enrolled about 7.2 million students in credit courses or about 40 percent of the total undergraduate student population, which was 17.7 million. These figures show that although community college enrollments increased significantly from 1979 to 2009 (by approximately 45 percent), the institution's share of the total undergraduate population has remained relatively stable.

Second, when considering the national community college student population, other details become significant (Knapp et al. 2011; Snyder and Dillow 2011). In 2009, community colleges enrolled 48 percent of the nation's African American undergraduate population and 58 percent of the Hispanic undergraduate population. Community colleges also enrolled 44 percent of the Asian/Pacific Islander student population and 50 percent of the Native American undergraduate population. Also, 46 percent of community college students receive some form of financial aid (federal, state, or institutional). These figures only confirm what many community college faculty and staff already know. That is, nationwide, community colleges enroll a disproportionate and higher share of minority students and students from low-income families when compared to 4-year colleges and universities.

Third, the enrollment of community college students—as part of the overall undergraduate population—varies significantly from state to state (Horn and Radwin 2012). So, for example, in states like Florida, North Dakota, South Dakota, and West Virginia, community colleges enroll less than 20 percent of the state's undergraduates. But, in states like California, Mississippi, New Mexico, and Wyoming, community colleges enroll more than 50 percent of the state's undergraduate student population. The reasons for these differences vary from state to state and they are usually the consequence of institutional and state history.

Fourth, student enrollment patterns are changing across higher education and this is also the case at community colleges. For instance, in the 1960s and 1970s, the dominant transfer pattern was one-way, that is, from the community college to the university or 4-year college. But there are an increasing number of post-baccalaureate reverse transfers (PBRTs) enrolling at community colleges. PBRTs are students with B.A. or B.S. degrees pursuing further study at a community college. Other enrollment patterns becoming more prevalent today are swirling and double-dipping (De los Santos and Sutton 2012; McCormick 2003). Swirling is the term used to describe students moving back and forth between two or more institutions to acquire courses needed for a degree. Double-dipping is how we refer to students enrolled concurrently at two or more institutions. These new enrollment patterns are posing serious challenges for all higher education institutions. When students enroll at two or more institutions while completing their college degree, no single institution has the ability to guide a student to completion. And, carrying this point forward, no single institution can be fairly credited or blamed for a student's success or failure.

What is noteworthy about these four considerations is this. Even though student enrollment patterns are unique in every state and at every campus, when viewed from a national perspective, community college student enrollments are increasing at a steady clip. And, these institutions continue to serve a disproportionate share of students from underrepresented minority and low-income populations. However, because student enrollment patterns are more varied than they were in the past, community colleges have less influence and control over their students. If state funding and federal financial aid programs become conditioned by student completion rates, this will pose serious challenges to all institutions, but especially community colleges, given the students they serve.

The community college mission

The traditional community college mission has three components and each is grounded in a philosophy of expanding educational opportunity (Cohen and Brawer 2008). The first is a commitment to open access. This commitment is reflected in the community college's "open door" admissions policy, its relatively low tuition, and the convenient delivery of courses and programs. Under the open door admissions policy, students are admitted to the college if they graduated from high school or passed the GED exam. Admission is not conditioned on a student's receiving a "minimum score" on standardized college tests (e.g., SAT or ACT). Nor do students need to produce a record of good high school grades. However, even when students have graduated from high school or passed the GED exam, they are usually required to take a placement test that assesses their ability in reading, writing, and mathematics. Students who cannot perform at college level on the placement test are usually required to refresh their skills or build them (if they were never acquired in high school) with developmental courses. The open door admissions policy ensures that any adult with the capacity to learn will be admitted to the college. But, then, if necessary, the student will be assigned to an educational program or curriculum to help develop the skills needed before beginning college level work.

Another dimension of open access is delivery of instructional programs and services at relatively low cost. At community colleges, the tuition and fees charged are typically less than those charged by public colleges and universities. And community college tuition and fees are much less than that charged by almost all private institutions (non profit and for-profit). For example, in 2011, the average published tuition and fees for full-time undergraduate students attending private non-profit institutions was $28,500. Similarly, the tuition and fees for full time, in-state undergraduate students attending a public university was $8,244. The tuition and fees for full time, in-state students enrolled at a community college was $2,963 (Baum and Ma 2011).

Finally, the commitment to open access is also exhibited through development of a course schedule that accommodates the needs of working adults. Typically, community colleges offer many programs on day and evening schedules. Similarly, community colleges demonstrate their commitment to access when they establish branch campuses and outreach centers so students can attend classes without traveling great distances. The relatively quick adoption of online learning at community colleges has been due in large measure to the institution's interest in providing greater access to students.

The second component of the community college mission is the commitment to deliver a "comprehensive" curriculum. When community college leaders say they are delivering a comprehensive curriculum, they usually mean their college offers three kinds of educational programs. First, they enroll students in 2-year associate in arts (A.A.) and associate in science (A.S.) degree programs. Students enrolled in these programs complete college level, credit-bearing courses and then transfer to a 4-year college or university where these transfer courses are used to satisfy the requirements of a bachelor's degree. Second, community colleges offer college-level, 1 and 2-year vocational programs. Students completing coursework for a 1-year program are awarded a certificate. Students completing a 2-year vocational program receive the associate in applied science (A.A.S.) degree. Community colleges award these credentials in a wide range of vocational areas, including architectural drafting, business administration, network administration, criminal justice, electronic engineering technology, nursing, respiratory technology, landscape technology, paralegal studies, and real estate sales. Students completing certificates and A.A.S. programs are expected to transition directly into the workforce with only limited on-the-job training. Third, community colleges offer a wide range of noncredit programs where students take (a) precollege, noncredit developmental courses in reading, writing, and mathematics to prepare for college level work, (b) noncredit adult education courses to acquire basic literacy skills (e.g., English as a Second Language), (c) short-term self-enrichment courses (e.g., photography, painting, and gardening), or (d) customized short-term training courses which are often marketed to employers.

The third component of the traditional mission is a commitment to serve the educational needs of the community where the college is located. This means that even though all community colleges offer a wide range of instructional programs, they tailor these to meet the educational needs of the communities they serve. Additionally, these institutions serve their communities by working closely with public schools, employers, the Chamber of Commerce, nearby higher education institutions, and nonprofit community groups (e.g., United Way).

As I mentioned earlier, the mission, or at least parts of it, are inscribed in state legislation that guides the operation of community colleges. However, local community college governing boards often adopt "missions statements" that incorporate the legislation and then provide a more detailed account of the institution's purpose. Mission statements are often prominently displayed on institutional websites, college catalogs, and other documents. The community college mission serves as a directive to the institution and its employees.

At this point, it is important to further clarify the difference between the institutional mission and an institution's normative vision. There are two important differences. First, as previously mentioned, in public higher education, authorities outside and above the institution set the institutional mission. An institution's mission can be debated and even challenged by the members of the organization. But, at the end of the day, the mission is established by the state legislature and governing authorities. A normative vision, on the other hand, is a matter of debate whether this occurs in formal or informal settings. It articulates the values and priorities that people in the college are asked to embrace. Second, an institution's mission helps distinguish it from other organizations. In the case of community colleges, the mission helps distinguish these institutions from 4-year colleges and universities. But the purpose of a normative vision is not to distinguish an institution from other related organizations. The purpose is to articulate the values and priorities that will guide the college.

At many community colleges, the institutional mission has become the *de facto* normative vision. That is, the values and priorities that guide faculty and staff coincide with the directive provided by the legislature and governing board. The coincidence of an institutional mission and normative vision is certainly understandable. But a college culture that limits its normative vision to the terms of its institutional mission is not making a commitment that goes beyond expanding educational opportunity. And, this can be problematic, especially when a portion of the college community believes the institution has an ethical duty to do more than expand educational opportunity. A question that runs throughout this book is what else *should* community colleges be doing? Almost all of us agree that community colleges should be expanding educational opportunity. Many of us agree that they should also be improving their completion rates. But should they aspire to do more than this? And, of course, my introduction of John Dewey into this conversation is for the purposes of explaining why, in addition to access and completion, community colleges should also promote individual growth and the development of democratic communities.

Community college funding

Historically, funding for community college operations came from three sources: state appropriations, local property or sales taxes, and student tuition (Cohen and Brawer 2008). The amount of funding community colleges received from any one of these three streams varied considerably from state to state.

And the same holds true today. Accordingly, today, in some states, community colleges receive up to 70 percent of their annual operational funding from state appropriations, with local taxes and student tuition accounting for the rest. In other states, community colleges now receive less than 10 percent of their annual funding from the state government, with the balance split between local taxes, student tuition, and other sources.

A critical aspect of any community college funding model concerns the manner in which state funding is allocated to individual colleges. Typically, in each state and in each regular legislative session, state legislatures appropriate a block of funding to a state community college coordinating agency, which then allocates funds to individual colleges. Traditionally, this allocation has been based on student enrollment. In the past, this kind of allocation provided a relatively easy and equitable way to distribute money to individual institutions. Community colleges that reported a significant enrollment increase from one year to the next would receive an increase in state funding to help cover the added expense of serving more students. Colleges that reported an enrollment decline would receive less. This funding system, based on changes to annual student enrollment, has been the dominant method of appropriating state funds to community colleges for 50 years (Cohen and Brawer 2008).

This process worked well from 1960 to 1990, when there was rough alignment between annual growth in community college student enrollment, the annual increase in state tax receipts, and the rising cost of state government programs and services. In other words, for many years, most states could increase state funding for community colleges (to pay for enrollment growth) so long as state tax revenue grew every year and the annual increase in the cost of other state programs (everything from K-12 education to corrections) remained in balance.

Beginning in the late 1980s and early 1990s, however, states were faced with three significant developments (Newman, Couturier and Scurry 2004: Roherty 1997). First, the cost of operating state corrections systems increased substantially from year to year. This increase was a consequence of the nation's unsuccessful war on drugs and the resulting incarceration of more people for minor drug offenses. Second, the states' share of federally subsidized health insurance for the poor (Medicaid) began to increase substantially. This increase was the consequence of the nation's inability to limit significant increases in the cost of health care and its failure to adopt an insurance model that might eventually bring these costs under control. Third, many but not all states began to adopt tax and expenditure limitations (TELs) that placed a limit on the collection of state tax revenue or state government expenditures. In some states, TELs placed a limit on the collection of state tax revenue *and* state government expenditures. TELs enabled state governments to slow down growth in appropriations for many state responsibilities, including public education and higher education.

When the cost of operating public colleges and universities exceeded the annual growth in state appropriations for these institutions, campus presidents and governing boards lobbied legislators to increase student tuition. In most cases, legislators were more than willing to pass along the increase in cost to students in the form of higher tuition. This regular ritual of limiting tax increases while approving tuition increases was how legislators satisfied taxpayers and campus presidents. But, of course, students, often those least capable of advocating effectively in state capitols, picked up the bill. This ritual also satisfied another critical priority, however, at least temporarily. It helped ensure that legislatures could maintain adequate levels of funding for corrections and Medicaid, two areas of state responsibility driven by outdated, expensive, and marginally effective public policy.

The pressure on state legislatures to limit growth in funding for higher education gradually changed the balance of revenue streams for all public institutions, including community colleges. It is important to note the magnitude of this change. In 1988, the states contributed approximately 58 percent of the funding supporting community colleges (Honeyman, Williamson and Wattenbarger 1991). But, by 2008 community colleges received only 30 percent of their total funding from state government appropriations (Palmer 2013).

Still, community colleges have been successful in limiting increases in student tuition, especially when compared to the tuition charged at other colleges and universities. For example, when researchers totaled up all of the revenues that United States higher education institutions collected nationwide, they found some interesting differences. In 2009, public 4-year colleges and universities collected 19 percent of their revenue from student tuition (Aud, Hussar, Johnson, Kena, Roth, Manning, Wang and Xhang 2012). Four-year private non profit institutions collected 33 percent of their revenue from student tuition and 4-year private for-profits collected 91 percent of their operating fund from students. American community colleges, on the other hand, collected only 16 percent of their revenue from students.

The discussion above only provides an overview of how community colleges are funded. Still, it explains why traditionally, when state appropriations were the single largest component of an institution's revenue stream, a state funding system based on student enrollment encouraged community colleges to increase enrollment. And this coincided perfectly with an institutional mission that emphasized educational opportunity. As state funding became more limited, and legislatures were unable to fully fund enrollment growth, enrollment-based funding models began to be viewed as something of a sham. That is, states were unable to hold to their own models in allocating funds to institutions. This led legislators to consider how other funding models might be used to allocate state funds to community colleges. It is hardly a coincidence that legislators' growing interest in the Completion Agenda has coincided with the need to move to funding models that consider factors besides enrollment, such as credential completion.

The Completion Agenda at the community college

In the Introduction, I described the Completion Agenda, the two economic justifications offered to support the reform movement, and AACC's 2012 endorsement of the policy in its report, *Reclaiming the American Dream*. Before proceeding further, however, a few more details about the Completion Agenda should be noted. To begin with, when viewed from a cultural perspective, the Completion Agenda is consistent with core beliefs many Americans have about education. We believe education can help solve social and economic problems (Grubb and Lazerson 2004; Labaree 2010). We also believe education is the best way for individuals to get ahead in society and achieve the American Dream. It is not surprising, therefore, that we might also believe that increasing the number of college graduates could improve the nation's economic performance, while also decreasing income inequality. Given this alignment with some of our core beliefs about education, we can see why the Completion Agenda is dominating many policy debates about education (Bragg and Durham 2012). But the Completion Agenda—a reform movement focused on attainment of a specific outcome—conflicts with another core belief. That is, Americans also believe that adults should have an opportunity to improve their lives through higher education, even if they lack a strong academic record or the ability to completely cover the cost of the education. And we believe they should have this opportunity even if they do not intend to complete a degree.

As intended by state legislators and education policymakers, community colleges have become the optimal starting place for many adults with a checkered academic record or limited financial resources. And, until recently, most legislatures were content with funding processes that rewarded educational opportunity but not student progress or graduation. Now, however, many state legislatures are examining proposals that, if enacted into law, would determine an institution's funding based, at least in part, on student progress and graduation rates. And state government commitments to both access and completion could easily lead to problems.

For example, in some states (e.g., Oregon), legislatures are pressuring community colleges to focus on completion, but still funding them based on enrollment (Fain 2013). In some cases, colleges have instituted programs to promote higher completion rates—such as limiting registration to students who are college-ready. But limiting registration in this manner is likely to lead to a decline in enrollment and, consequently, the colleges may suffer a financial penalty for adopting a completion strategy.

Additionally, the pressure to increase completion rates may tempt community college administrators to divert students away from 2-year associate degrees and into 1-year certificate programs because of the higher probability of completion. Because these certificate programs tend to be in vocational areas, community colleges may be accused, yet again, of diverting students into short-term vocational programs and out of longer programs leading to the B.A. or B.S. degrees (Brint and Karabel 1989; Clark 1960a).

Finally, a push for higher enrollments in short-term vocational education programs might have positive financial consequences for community colleges. But it may provide graduates only with a temporary benefit. In some cases, a strong general education is a more certain predictor of employment in later life than vocational training that may become outdated (Hanushek, Woessmann and Zhang 2011; Humphreys 2012).

What also remains problematic is how the Completion Agenda will be advanced in the years ahead. Although private foundations and advocacy groups will have a major role in proposing institutional strategies, state and federal governments will have the greatest power to drive the reform through direct and indirect subsidization of colleges and universities. Because the funding of higher education is inherently political, making specific predictions at this time on how the Completion Agenda will play out is impossible.

To be sure, the goals of improving economic competitiveness and reducing income inequality are important national economic objectives. However, for a variety of reasons, community colleges may be the guinea pigs for a set of policies that carry not only significant promise but also significant risk. Community colleges are already the most vocational institutions in American higher education (Grubb and Lazerson 2004). They already have the facilities, the faculty, and the partnerships with business and industry to move toward even greater vocationalization. Compared to 4-year colleges and universities, community colleges are also less encumbered by a culture that privileges faculty autonomy. Change and even radical change, for better or worse, is more likely at the community college. It would be a tragic irony, however, if the Completion Agenda pushed community colleges to become even more vocationalized, achieve goals driven by national economic policies, but then deprived students of an opportunity to live richer lives and play a greater role in the American democracy. In summary, it is easy to see why some critics contend the Completion Agenda is likely to continue the social stratification of American higher education, leaving many community college students on the sidelines (e.g., Rhoades 2012).

The need for a new normative vision

Community colleges should certainly work harder to improve student access. They should also improve their completion rates. But the community college of the future needs to do much more than this. As I argue later, twenty-first-century community colleges need to become much more student and community focused. They need to help individual adult learners grow not just vocationally, but as members of their community. Community colleges also need to take a stronger leadership role in developing democratic communities through what they do best—helping solve community problems through education.

The development of democratic communities through education, as envisioned by Dewey, is not some utopian project. It does not entail adopting a radical ideology or a foreign way of life. It is simply the incremental process of helping people better understand the problems facing their communities and then, in collaboration with others, developing solutions that promote personal growth. This perspective, which emphasizes learning from our own experience, developing shared interests, and problem solving in collaboration with others, would not require some radical reconstruction of the community college, its curricula, or student support services. Campus parking would still be a problem. But, it would help community colleges ensure that while students are completing their courses and programs, they are also acquiring the knowledge and skills needed to create a better democracy.

In order to develop this new vision, however, we must first understand how community colleges came to focus on educational opportunity. We also need to understand why they are seen by many today as the ideal institution to play a major role in increasing credential completion. In other words, we need to understand how community colleges became local institutions focused on achieving national priorities.

More than other American higher education institutions, community colleges have struggled to establish their own unique and positive identity within the American higher education hierarchy. In Chapters 4, 5, 6, and 7, I review this history. In these chapters I show that the evolution of junior colleges and community colleges was much more tentative, ambiguous, and uncertain than many of us might think. Traditional community college advocates, however, prefer to tell another story. They prefer to portray the institution as one that was destined to take its place in the American higher education hierarchy and one that has enjoyed many successes and few setbacks. This positive picture draws a straight line from the small junior college in the early twentieth century to the large complex multi-campus community college of the early twenty-first century. The record shows, however, that the development of these institutions was not so certain and not so rosy. In fact, for many decades, educational leaders and researchers argued about what junior colleges (and later, community colleges) should do and even where they should be located in the education hierarchy. These contingencies, however, are not a part of the conventional history of how community colleges developed.

The conventional history

The conventional history of community colleges is inscribed in books and articles. This history is also part of the institutional culture at many community colleges and whether encountered in print or in conversation, it goes something like this: the first community colleges began operating in the early 1900s. They were established in the Midwest and West, where there were very few colleges and universities. Enlightened community leaders created these institutions to provide high school graduates with an opportunity to complete college level courses while staying at home. There were only one or two community colleges operating in 1900 and their total enrollment was less than 200 students. But, by 2000, their numbers had increased to more than 1,100 and these institutions served more than 6 million. As we might expect, the community college curriculum changed over time. In the early 1900s, the major focus of these institutions was on delivering courses for transfer to the university. But over the next 40 years, many took on responsibility for delivering adult vocational education programs as well.

Each college developed in accordance with local needs and interests. The growth in the number of colleges and also in student enrollment reflected the good fit between community college programs and the educational needs of a changing society and growing economy. Community colleges experienced a major increase in enrollment after World War II, when returning veterans went to college to acquire the skills needed to secure employment, start up a business, or take over the family farm. During the 1960s, community colleges played a major role in enrolling women and minorities, two populations traditionally excluded from many higher education institutions. Most recently, community colleges have been the institution of choice for immigrants seeking to make a new life in America.

The conventional history reminds us that community colleges enroll a substantial minority of all undergraduate students. They offer a wide range of programs to meet the educational needs of the community. Community colleges have been a steady and reliable partner to schools, universities, and employers, always ready to meet the educational needs of the community. They are a uniquely American institution—committed to expanding educational opportunity. And, when community colleges provide these services, they contribute to the future success of the nation. These sentiments were captured in the AACC 2012 report, *Reclaiming the American Dream,* when the authors wrote, "Community colleges, an American invention, are one of the greatest assets of this nation in the task of creating a better future" (AACC 2012, p. viii).

The conventional history tells us that the success of these institutions was due in large measure to serving educational needs that were not addressed by 4-year colleges and universities. These institutions had their own purposes and missions and they followed their own paths. During the seventeenth, eighteenth, and nineteenth centuries, small private liberal arts colleges took on the role of educating the children of privilege, awarding undergraduate degrees, and producing community leaders informed by the great works of Western civilization. During the late nineteenth and early twentieth centuries, new public universities accepted the responsibility of advancing science, awarding undergraduate and graduate degrees, and enrolling the most capable students in the state. In the early twentieth century, community college leaders recognized and exploited an opportunity for growth by offering the first 2 years of an undergraduate education to students unable to attend liberal arts colleges and universities. Later in the twentieth century, enrollment growth continued when these leaders offered new adult vocational educational programs. The conventional history tells us, therefore, that throughout the twentieth century, community college enrollments grew and then secured their status by identifying and then satisfying unmet needs in higher education. The institutional identity that emerged, therefore, was grounded in a mission and vision of expanding educational opportunity. This mission and vision lasted until the first decade of the twenty-first century. Then, the Financial Crisis and Great Recession led many Americans to openly wonder if the nation was on a long slow road to decline. Policy makers and educators, eager to counter this anxiety and fear, argued successfully for a new mission and normative vision for community colleges, one that would transform the institution so it can focus on the most important economic needs of the nation. Where this mission and normative vision will take community colleges, should it remain in place, is an open question. What is clear, however, is that community colleges have arrived at a crossroads and their future remains unknown.

Conclusion

The American community college is a central player in the higher education hierarchy. It enrolls approximately 40 percent of the total undergraduate student population. Community colleges are able to serve this large population at a reasonable cost because of the support they receive from the state, federal, and local governments. In many respects, nearby and inexpensive community colleges are a dream come true for many students. However, their low completion rates have made them a prime target for politicians and policymakers. Thus, community colleges are being torn between their traditional commitment to access and a new expectation of higher completion rates. This new chapter in the history of community college education caps a conventional history that has consistently emphasized institutional growth and student access.

The conventional history that I shared above is true. But there is much more to the story than what this history tells us. These additional details are critically important and must be considered if we are to understand how and why an institution committed to expanding educational opportunity would move so quickly to change and align its operations with national economic policy. Before turning to these details, however, I need to describe important drivers that will shape the environment community colleges will occupy in the decades ahead. Discussion of a new normative vision needs to acknowledge the institution's past. But, it also needs to account for the conditions that will significantly influence the evolution of community college education in the future.

2

The community college
of the future

Introduction

Like all higher education institutions, community colleges exist in a complex
and constantly changing environment. Any discussion about developing
a new normative vision must acknowledge this environment. There are five
drivers that will significantly influence the evolution of higher education
and community colleges in particular. These are (a) income inequality,
(b) technological change and learning analytics, (c) globalization, (d) the
generational equity problem, and (e) public higher education funding. These
drivers are interrelated and each affects the operation of community colleges
in different ways. Distilling them out here as distinct factors inevitably limits
our appreciation of their complexity. However, a description of each, as an
independent driver, helps illuminate its essential aspects.

Income inequality

The American higher education policy and practitioner communities are well
aware of recent analyses reporting on the nation's growing income inequality
(e.g., Duncan and Murnane 2011; Goldin and Katz 2009). In examining this
inequality, Completion Agenda advocates often focus on the difference in
earnings between college graduates and those who only hold a high school
diploma. Researchers have found that across the board, for all the major ethnic
groups and for both men and women, more education means a higher income
(Baum, Ma and Payea 2013). Completion Agenda advocates believe this
explains why improving college graduation rates will reduce income inequality.
There is certainly data to support this belief. However, it may also be true that
income inequality is being driven by independent economic factors that may

not be affected by higher college completion rates (Piketty 2014). And, to get a better grasp on this possibility, it helps to first focus on the magnitude of the nation's income and wealth inequality problem (Goldin and Katz 2009; Piketty 2014; Piketty and Saez 2013; Stiglitz 2012).

When we examine family income by population grouping, that is by "decile" (e.g., the top 10 percent, the bottom 10 percent), the growth since the late 1970s has gone disproportionately to the highest income earning families (Piketty and Saez 2013). Thus, for example, the top 10 percent received approximately 35 percent of all income in the late 1970s but by 2008 this group received almost 50 percent of all income. Similarly, the top 1 percent of families received just under 10 percent of all income in the late 1970s but by 2008 this group received almost 20 percent of all income.

In a nation where income or money is used to purchase influence in the political system, this inequality represents a direct threat to the notion of representative democracy. In other words, although Americans believe in the "one person, one vote" principle, this principle loses much of its meaning if a very small portion of the population can purchase influence, television ads, campaign or referendum workers, and research reports on controversial issues. Of course, this inequality in income has consequences that go beyond the political dimension of our democracy. In the United States, K-12 education, higher education, health care, police services, and basic food and clothing are all distributed based on the consumer's income. A high level of income inequality not only means that the top 10 percent of income earners have great purchasing power. It means the bottom 90 percent (and especially those in the bottom decile) have much less.

Three other points need to be considered in assessing the significance of income inequality. First, a focus on income inequality does not tell us a great deal about the nation's inequality in wealth. Because wealth is amassed and invested in ways that are often difficult to track, we must accept that the inequality in income, which is more transparent and easier to track through income tax laws, may be much less than inequality in wealth.

Second, income inequality in the United States is greater than that found in most European countries and Japan. Although the top 1 percent of American families earned almost 20 percent of income in 2008, only the United Kingdom had a similar disparity. In 2008, the top 1 percent of families in Germany, the Netherlands, Japan, Sweden, France, and Switzerland all received between 5 and 12 percent of the nation's income. Completion advocates may be correct in claiming that an increase in college completers will help limit the increasing inequality of income in the United States. What has limited income inequality in many other nations, however, has been a much more progressive income tax.

Third, and finally, a review of income inequality in the United States over the last 100 years confirms that the current high inequality has only existed during one previous period and that was from 1920 to 1940. Then, the richest 10 percent enjoyed the benefits of the Roaring 1920s and many escaped the worst of the Great Depression in the 1930s. Coincidentally, this is roughly the period in which John Dewey produced some of his most detailed writings on democracy and his most critical texts on American society. It is hardly surprising that so many are now focusing on income inequality as a major threat to the nation's democracy. What has yet to be adequately explained, of course, is why state and federal governments are focusing on college completion, almost exclusively, as the sole remedy for the income inequality problem. As I explain later, Dewey had other ideas.

Technological change and learning analytics

The second driver has two components: (a) innovations in information and communication technologies (ICT) and (b) advancements in quantitative social sciences, commonly referred to as "Big Data." The emergence of this driver raises the possibility that over the next 10 years, teaching and learning might become much more accessible, flexible, personalized, and manageable. Examples of ICT innovations include more sophisticated learning management systems, e-portfolio systems, online virtual worlds (e.g., Second Life), social media (e.g., Facebook and Twitter), social platforms (e.g., Flickr and YouTube), and Massive Open Online Courses (MOOCs).

The primary significance of the ICT innovations is that they are radically altering the way we live, work, consume, and learn. As Terry O'Banion observed almost 20 years ago, most of higher education is still using a nineteenth century, agrarian era model to organize teaching and learning (O'Banion 1997). O'Banion could make the same point today. The traditional model assumes learning is best organized in synchronous class sessions over 16-week semesters in the fall and spring. The model also holds that the instructor's primary responsibility is to deliver content and evaluate student work products. The responsibility to support and guide actual learning is negligible. This model persists, however, because it can be easily used to measure student enrollment growth, which in turn helps justify institutional requests for increased state funding.

Learning analytics is another part of this driver. By learning analytics, I refer to the large scale, systematic collection, analysis, and interpretation of learning interactions that may be used to measure and then assess the effectiveness of the teaching and learning process (Bishop 2012; Greller and Drachsler 2012).

The use of learning analytics is typically understood in the context of ICTs. But the philosophy behind it is not. The reasonable assumption behind learning analytics is that effective data mining and analysis of learning interactions will lead to insights concerning the best environments and conditions for supporting and assessing individual student's learning. So long as data can be systematically collected, stored, and analyzed, learning analytics could help instructors improve student mastery of everything from humanities courses to avalanche safety trainings in the field. Learning analytics is becoming a more common tool in higher education and has the potential to significantly improve student learning while also emphasizing the development of creative intelligence (Bishop 2012; Greller and Drachsler 2012). Although its widespread use has not yet occurred and its long term costs remain unknown, the educational potential of this innovation is promising. And this promise is especially appealing to community colleges because of their prioritization of teaching and learning. Learning analytics may not increase community college enrollments. But it could help increase completion rates.

Globalization

Globalization is the third driver that will affect higher education institutions in the future. Globalization is best understood as the creation, integration, and intensification of economic, political, social, and bioecological systems in ways that have a significant effect on our lives (Brynjolfsson and McAfee 2011; Goldin 2013; Held and McGrew 2007; Rodrik 2011; Sassen 2007). It is the consequence of many conditions but advancements in digital technologies, the electronic movement of capital, and new global transportation networks are the most important. Globalization is usually regarded as a phenomenon operating across national boundaries. But it can also operate within nations. One consequence of globalization is that people are now more interconnected than ever and this provides new opportunities for communication, shared understanding, and trade.

There are many advantages to globalization when we think of ourselves as consumers or entrepreneurs. As consumers, globalization provides us with a wider range of products and services available for quick or immediate purchase (e.g., mobile phones, electronics, and digital media). These in turn become a part of our lives, offering new conveniences and entertainment. As entrepreneurs, globalization provides us with new opportunities to design, market, and sell products and services to a world-wide market.

But, of course, globalization is not innocuous, especially when we consider ourselves as workers. Globalization permits investors and managers to make instantaneous changes in the production of goods and services in order to lower costs, maximize profits, and expand market share. This can include diverting work from one factory to another in a matter of hours. Because international regulation of the global economy is still underdeveloped, corporations can prioritize economic gain with only limited attention to fair wages, workplace safety, and the environment (Goldin 2013). When corporations move work from one location to another, the resulting unemployment and forced migration can devastate communities and families. In a globalized world, we are all much more likely to experience these workplace changes.

Another aspect of this problem is that globalization is creating more economic inequality between nations and also within nations (Goldin 2013). We see this in the United States. Workers with limited skills are more easily pushed into unemployment when their jobs are shipped overseas to a cheaper workforce. And, in many industries today, the jobs being created are qualitatively inferior to those of the past. More work has become automated, reducing the need for full-time employees. Therefore employers are also hiring more part-time workers, without traditional benefits.

Traditionally, community colleges have played an important role in helping consumers adapt to new technologies (e.g., teaching adults how to use new software programs). They also have a long history in helping entrepreneurs start new businesses. However, because the nation is now experiencing chronic unemployment, underemployment, and increasing income inequality, community colleges will also be working with a growing part of the population that may never be able to fully participate in the twenty-first-century global economy. In the past, laid off workers could come to the community college with some assurance that retraining would lead to a new job, somewhere in the community. Our new chronically unemployed and underemployed cannot be so optimistic.

Globalization is also changing the business of higher education. This creates new opportunities for community colleges but also new liabilities. The opportunities include the ability to expand enrollments through the use of ICT technologies. They also include the potential for colleges and universities to share and synthesize curricula. These opportunities existed in the past. But, in the digital world, the impediments to these innovations are cultural or institutional and not technological. Again, however, there is a downside to higher education and community colleges. The best example of this downside is the rapid enrollment growth for private for-profit institutions, many of which operate almost entirely online with faculties that are predominately part-time. For community colleges, this new competition from institutions often thousands of miles away, represents a threat to their enrollment and, therefore, budget stability.

Finally, globalization will have another important effect on community colleges. Over the next 10 years, the Asia-Pacific region will become the most powerful region of consumers in the world economy (Kharas 2010; Mahbubani 2013). This rising dominance of the Asia-Pacific region as the most powerful consumer region in the world is reflected in these numbers. In 2009, 54 percent of the global middle class (households spending an equivalent of $10 to $100 a day) were in North America and Europe and 28 percent were in the Asia-Pacific region (Kharas 2010). However, by 2020, North America and Europe are expected to have only 32 percent of the global middle class while the Asia-Pacific region will have 53 percent. A rapidly expanding middle class in the Asia-Pacific region will require a sophisticated workforce in order to maintain this new higher quality of life. Countries in the region are quickly increasing their capacity to develop this workforce. China had 1,022 higher educational institutions in 2001 and by 2010 it had 2,263 (Mahbubani 2013). But even this kind of growth will not provide the capacity needed to prepare all qualified Chinese students for middle class lives at home or around the world. Accordingly, a significant increase in the enrollment of international students at American colleges and universities, especially from the Asia-Pacific region, will continue for at least another 10 to 20 years. In fact, this increased enrollment in the United States of students from Asia is happening now. The number of Chinese studying in American colleges and universities increased from 100,000 in 2008 to over 157,000 by 2010 (Mahbubani 2013). These numbers suggest that American higher education still retains an excellent reputation across the globe and will remain highly sought after by young people who demonstrate exceptional promise to their governments and families.

Because the higher education industry is very status conscious and always seeking new revenue, American 4-year colleges and universities will continue to enroll more high quality and affluent students from the Asia-Pacific region. However, at some institutions this will limit access for domestic students. A cascading effect could force American students into community colleges who, in earlier years, would have gained admission at other colleges and universities. The rise of the middle class in the Asia-Pacific region could also increase enrollments at community colleges for another reason. If a significant portion of these new international students need remediation or improved English language skills before beginning advanced undergraduate work, the community college may gain an even larger share of this market. To be sure, the United States will see an increase in international students coming from all parts of the world. But the Asia-Pacific region, because of the size of its population and strong economy, will affect all sectors of American higher education and almost certainly, community colleges as well.

In summary, the consequences of globalization for community colleges are best assessed as substantial but variable. In some cases these could increase enrollment and strengthen the institution's financial standing. But, in others, the institution could suffer a significant loss of revenue and students. Globalization, therefore, must be regarded as a major factor likely to influence community colleges but in ways that may vary greatly from one institution to the next or from one community to the next.

The problem of generational equity

A fourth driver that will inevitably affect the future of community college education is generational inequity (Taylor & Pew Research Center 2014). As Paul Taylor and his colleagues at the Pew Research Center have shown, the United States is now challenged by a series of problems rooted in the generational inequities that have developed over the last 50 years. At the heart of these problems is a series of governmental programs and policies that directly or indirectly benefit older Americans at the expense of younger Americans. The prime examples are the federal government's Social Security and Medicare programs. These programs provide older Americans with financial benefits that substantially exceed what they and their employers contributed while they were working. The problem of course, is not that the federal government established these programs, nor is it one of entitlement. We can stipulate that every humane society has a responsibility to care for its older and infirm citizens. The underlying problem is that life expectancy has increased far beyond what Congress anticipated when it enacted Social Security in 1935 and Medicare in 1965. Consequently, the programs provide older Americans with direct financial support and health care insurance coverage for a much longer period of time than initially intended.

Today, working taxpayers are paying a larger share of the cost for these programs, there are a decreasing number of workers and an increasing number of beneficiaries, and younger Americans are unlikely to ever see comparable benefits when they retire. Although Social Security and Medicare are the leading examples of this inequity, the federal, state, and local governments also provide a wide range of other social services and tax benefits to older Americans (e.g., tax exemptions and reduced fees for services) heavily subsidized by younger Americans.

The consequences of these generational inequities are many but two are especially important to the future of community colleges and their students. First, the federal, state, and local governments are failing to make greater investments in programs and services benefitting younger Americans in order to follow through on social programs that disproportionately benefit older Americans. These neglected programs and services include subsidized childcare, juvenile corrections, public education (K-12 schools), and public higher education (community colleges and public 4-year colleges and universities). If programs and services benefitting older Americans were less expensive or means-tested, the federal, state, and local governments would have more revenue available to spend on programs and services that community college students are likely to access. Similarly, if governments levied higher taxes, at progressive rates, on income and wealth, they would also have more revenue to subsidize services that disproportionately benefit the young. To date, of course, most governments have declined to means test these services or raise revenue.

Second, perhaps the most obvious example of generational inequity in a higher education context, is the student loan crisis. Sustained funding for programs benefitting older Americans has resulted in less funding for colleges and universities and also less funding for student financial aid, especially in the form of need-based financial aid grants. But the student loan crisis is also a consequence of (a) higher education, as an industry, failing to control its costs, (b) state legislatures rubber-stamping tuition increases proposed by public institutions, and (c) states moving resources out of need-based grant programs and into student loan programs (Baum and Ma 2011; Baum and Payea 2011; Baum, Payea and Steele 2009).

Awareness of the student loan crisis exploded in May 2012 when Martin and Lehren wrote a front page story for the *New York Times* recounting a series of student debtor horror stories (Martin and Lehren 2012). For many Americans, this was their first introduction to the problem and its dimensions were shocking. Martin and Lehren explained how the nation's total student loan debt, at approximately $1 trillion, exceeded the nation's total credit card debt. And, they explained, the average student loan debt in 2011 "was $23,300, with 10 percent owing more than $54,000 and 3 percent more than $100,000" (Martin and Lehren 2012, p. 1). When this debt is measured by household, the amount owed has tripled since 1989 and the number of households owing student loans has increased by more than 100 percent during this same period.

The consequence of the student loan crisis is that many students are delaying starting a family, buying a home, and starting up a business because of a lack of income. The student loan crisis will hold many students back in their quest to become independent and get on with their lives. For community colleges, however, the crisis represents another unknown. Some colleges may experience increased enrollment pressure from students unwilling or unable to bear the debt associated with a more expensive college education. Others may face pressure to adopt baccalaureate programs in order to provide a new less expensive path to attaining this credential. In any event, the student crisis will have ripple effects throughout higher education that could alter a community college's intended path.

Public funding for higher education

A fifth driver is public higher education funding. This is closely related to the problem of generational equity and governments' curtailment of funding for public colleges and universities to support programs benefitting older Americans. Three points raise grave concerns about the prospects for state and federal financing for public higher education over the next 20 years.

To begin with, although student enrollment in public colleges and universities has steadily increased over the last 10 years, the states' share of the funding for these institutions is dropping. Earlier, in Chapter 1, I noted that the states' contribution to the community college operational budget had declined significantly since 1988. This development has affected all of public higher education and the decline has been particularly sharp over the last 6 years. In March 2013, the Center on Budget and Policy Priorities reported that state funding of public higher education had dropped precipitously from 2008 (Oliff, Palacios, Johnson and Leachman 2013). When compared to what was spent in 2008, only two of the 50 states were spending more, when calculated on a per-student basis. On average, the states had decreased funding for public higher education, on a per student basis, by 28 percent. This decline, accelerated by the Financial Crisis and the Great Recession, has shifted a higher share of the cost of acquiring a higher education to students. This shift is troubling because it follows 30 years of stagnation in median household income (Mishel, Bivens, Gould and Shierholz 2012). In other words, although most students and their families have not experienced a real increase in income, they are being asked to pay more in tuition and fees.

Looking ahead, there are many unknowns when we try to anticipate future levels and models of state funding for community colleges. What seems certain, however, is that for a variety of reasons, it is unlikely that community colleges will see a significant increase in state funding. In fact, most community colleges will probably be asked, again, to do more with less.

Second, the federal government's ability to continue funding higher education at current levels is uncertain. On this point, it is important to note that traditionally, the two largest areas of federal funding for higher education are research and student financial aid. In 2008, the federal government provided approximately $31 billion to American 4-year colleges and universities (public and private) for research (College Board Advocacy and Policy Center 2013;

Matthews 2012). Community colleges, without a research mission, received essentially zero dollars for research from the federal government. Also, in 2008, American 4-year colleges and universities (public and private) received approximately $13.3 billion from the federal government in the form of student financial aid grants (the majority of which is awarded based on need). American community colleges received $5.9 billion from the federal government in the form of student financial aid grants.

Unfortunately, the federal government's ability to maintain its current levels of support for higher education—for any purpose and for any sector—is in doubt. There are two reasons for this.

First, as noted earlier, over the last 13 years, the federal government's serious debt problem has become much worse. The wars in Iraq and Afghanistan created long-term financial and human consequences already surpassing the government's ability to adequately manage. Also, the federal government's costs for recovery from the Financial Crisis and Great Recession have added more debt to the ledger. The consequence of these developments, as I have noted, is that although the nation's total accumulated federal debt in September 2007 was $9 trillion, by November 2013 it was $17 trillion (United States Treasury Department, TreasuryDirect, Historical Debt Outstanding 2012).

Second, the federal debt is being financed by the sale of United States Treasury notes and bonds that, to date, have been marketed with low interest rates, that is, with low cost to the borrower, the US federal government. The big question is, how long will the federal government be able to sell these low interest notes and bonds to raise revenue to meet its financial obligations? Since a third of the annual federal budget is now covered through borrowing, this is not an academic question. If interest rates increase significantly and the federal government is unable to borrow large amounts of money as it has in the past, funding for research and financial aid programs could drop precipitously. This would have a significant negative impact on much of the American society, including community colleges and their students.

In conclusion, a related consideration also needs to be noted. We often think of American higher education as being an essentially public enterprise. But this was not always the case. Private institutions dominated American higher education for most of the nation's history. Excepting a brief period during the Great Depression, public colleges and universities did not enroll most college students until 1952 (Snyder 1993). From that date forward, public institutions have consistently enrolled a majority of college students. However, there has been an important shift in student enrollment over the past 10 years. From 1970 to 2000, public institutions enrolled approximately 70 percent of the total student population. Beginning in 2004, however, private institutions (including the expanding for-profit sector) began to enroll a larger share of the student population. In that year, private institutions enrolled 33 percent of college students. This increased to 35 percent in 2006 and then 37 percent in 2008. In 2010, private institutions increased their share of the total college student population to 38 percent (Snyder and Dillow 2011).

Community colleges are public institutions that rely heavily on public funding—directly from state and local governments and indirectly from the federal government. However, the significant increase in enrollments at private institutions over the last 10 years represents a shift that cannot be entirely explained at this point in time. Even though community college enrollments continue to increase nationwide, the increase in enrollments at private institutions could eventually divert government funding from the public sector to the private sector, especially if private institutions (both for-profit and nonprofit) become perceived as better end users of these resources. This development may seem unlikely now. But if private institutions demonstrate an ability to become more responsive to government priorities than public institutions, the recent shift in the distribution of student enrollments between public and private institutions could accelerate.

Conclusion

In summary, the five drivers discussed above will have a significant impact on the environment within which community colleges and their students exist. Each will pressure community colleges to change in significant ways and several have possible consequences for the Completion Agenda. Some of these drivers (e.g., income inequality, generational inequity, uncertain public funding for higher education) will probably place community colleges and their students in more precarious financial circumstances. For example, if we continue on our current path, increasing income inequality and generational inequities may mean the society will reduce its allocations for social services benefitting low-income students. Financial aid may be drastically reduced. Students' ability to progress and graduate may be compromised by reduced funding for college support programs. Globalization may provide students with significant advantages as consumers but may also pose significant threats to their long-term employment prospects. These developments are especially hard to predict. Finally, technological change and learning analytics may offer students and the colleges greater flexibility and capacity to support learning. But many of these innovations are still at the pilot stage and not in use at most colleges.

As community colleges prepare for the future, the one conclusion that seems to rise from a consideration of each driver is that the state and federal governments may be less likely to help manage this environment. In short, it would be naive to assume that the cavalry will be coming over the hill to save community colleges. Therefore, the transformation of community colleges into more effective and efficient institutions will probably be the result of closer relationships with constituents and more active engagement with their communities.

The development of more productive relationships will not be the great challenge here. The primary task will be building and then adhering to the values and priorities needed for this transformation, that is, developing the vision needed to guide the institution to recommit to its local partners. Of course, they too will be challenged by some of the drivers. The task, therefore, will be building a better community in which community colleges do more for their students and constituents while the community and constituents do more for the institution and its students. And the business of building better communities, better democratic communities, leads us to John Dewey.

3

Introducing John Dewey

Introduction

In this chapter, I offer an overview of John Dewey's life, highlighting his experiences while working at the University of Chicago and Columbia University. This account sets the stage for a closer review of his works in Chapters 8, 9, and 10. In these later chapters, I show how Dewey's writings provide the building blocks for a normative vision for the twenty-first-century community college. These texts, of course, were shaped by his life experiences. Accordingly, in order to understand the conclusions Dewey came to in later life, we need to see where and how he lived. This chapter provides this introduction.

Dewey's early years

Dewey was born on October 20, 1859 in Burlington, Vermont. When the Civil War broke out in 1861 his father, a shopkeeper, joined the First Vermont Cavalry as a quartermaster and was away for most of the conflict (Dykhuizen 1973). Dewey's mother held the family together for 3 years during his absence. But in 1864, she moved her three children to northern Virginia to be closer to her husband. We do not have any reliable firsthand accounts of Dewey's childhood experiences during the war. But his intellectual biographers noted it had a great impact on him (e.g., Hook 1939; Menand 2001).

For example, Menand wrote that the Civil War provided Dewey with important insights into human society (Menand 2001). One of these was that when a nation is divided by a deep controversy and the political process cannot resolve it, violence is always possible. Another insight was that rigid identification with a partisan group or region of the country makes compromise extremely difficult. Third, Dewey learned that life is inescapably contingent. Hardship, tragedy, illness, and death are always a risk. Finally, because the Civil War was a conflict that could have been avoided, Dewey understood the importance of helping children and then adults learn how to work with one another to solve problems, no matter how challenging or divisive they might appear.

After the Civil War ended, the Dewey family returned to Burlington. In the late 1860s, the city was changing socially and economically as it became a center for newly mechanized lumber mills. The mills employed many people in difficult and dangerous jobs. Immigrants, unable to secure other employment, often ended up working in these mills (Ryan 1995). Dewey was more fortunate than many of these immigrants and he enrolled at the University of Vermont in 1875, focusing on the classics, a common course of study at that time. He graduated with a bachelor's degree in 1879 and then left Vermont to work as a high school teacher in Oil City, Pennsylvania (Dykhuizen 1973; Ryan 1995). Dewey was not satisfied with this experience or life in the small town of Oil City and he returned to Vermont in 1881, accepting a position as a high school teacher at the Lake View Seminary in Charlotte. Still disappointed with the life of a teacher, in the summer of 1882 he left Vermont and began graduate study in the philosophy department at Johns Hopkins University in Baltimore, Maryland. He received his Ph.D. in 1884.

Despite Dewey's accomplishments in later life, his success as an academic was far from certain when he began his doctoral studies. His speaking voice was dull. His physical appearance was often unimpressive. In 1883, the presidents of Johns Hopkins University and the University of Vermont discussed Dewey's future in an exchange of letters. Both men knew Dewey personally and both had reservations about his future as a professor (Hickman 2008, *Introduction to Dewey's Correspondence Volume 1, 1871–1918*). Gilman, President at the University of Vermont, observed that Dewey was "reserved" and wondered whether the mild-mannered young man had sufficient "pedagogic power" to hold the attention of a class of undergraduate students. Buckham, the Johns Hopkins President, was not sure if Dewey had the "amount of dogmatism that a teacher ought to have" (Letter from D. C. Gilman to M. H. Buckham, March 30, 1883, (00428); Letter from M. H. Buckham to D. C. Gilman, April 3, 1883, (00426)).

Nevertheless, Dewey pursued an academic career and after leaving Johns Hopkins went on to teach at the University of Michigan in the fall of 1884. While in Ann Arbor, Dewey met and married Alice Chipman in 1886, just weeks after she graduated from the University of Michigan with a bachelor's degree in philosophy. The young couple left Ann Arbor in the summer of 1888, when John accepted a position at the University of Minnesota. Dewey returned to Michigan in 1889, however, and remained there for the next five years. In 1894, Dewey moved again after accepting a position at the University of Chicago, a new university established by the oil baron, John D. Rockefeller. The University of Chicago was led by a young and ambitious president, William Rainey Harper. Harper appointed Dewey as professor and head of the Philosophy Department (Letter from John Dewey to William Rainey Harper, March 19, 1894, (00501)). This move would prove to be a life-changing experience for Dewey, not just because of his scholarly accomplishments at the university but because of what he saw in the streets of Chicago.

The Chicago years

During the last decade of the nineteenth century and the first decade of the twentieth century, Chicago was a city of 1.7 million people undergoing great social change (Grossman, Keating and Reiff 2004; Miller 1996). In 1900, the city was a community of migrants with 35 percent of its population foreign-born and another 43 percent with at least one parent born outside the United States. During these years, Chicago was also the arena in which large corporations and large labor unions battled. Labor strikes and employer lockouts were common.

As an example, in 1893, the nation fell into a deep recession when railroad companies overbuilt and then realized that their passenger and freight revenues were insufficient to pay down the massive debt incurred during the construction. The railroad companies pared down their purchases of equipment and supplies and this triggered a decline in the nation's economy. The Pullman Palace Car Company, located in Pullman, Illinois, just outside Chicago, saw a decline in orders for new railroad cars. This led to a reduction in the wages for Pullman employees. In some cases, weekly wages declined by 50 percent. The impact of these cuts was exacerbated by a company-town system that left the Pullman employees in debt to their employer for rent and grocery bills. In the spring of 1894, with the support of Eugene V. Debs, a leader of the American Railway Union, the Pullman workers organized a local union and in May they struck (Lindsey 1942; Salvatore 1982).

When the Pullman Palace Car Company rejected arbitration with the striking workers, the Union ordered a boycott. This precipitated a national crisis as rail traffic was interrupted when railway workers across the country refused to service the Pullman cars. The *New York Times* described the unfolding conflict as one that would be "probably the greatest strike" in US history (*New York Times*, July 1, 1894, p. 1). And, the newspaper reported, the unrest was "the beginning of what is expected to be the greatest struggle between capital and labor ever inaugurated in the United States" (*New York Times*, June 27, 1894, p. 8). This prediction was not an exaggeration. At its height, the strike in Chicago and the boycott across the country affected 27 states with 250,000 workers participating.

Lawyers for the Pullman Company worked closely with the US attorney general (a former member of several railroad corporate governing boards) and on July 3 two federal court judges issued an injunction declaring the strike illegal, as an unlawful interference with the US mail (Salvatore 1982). President Grover Cleveland ordered 2,000 federal troops to the scene and they began to arrive in Chicago by the evening of July 3rd. Violence and rioting followed in Chicago and then at other railroad facilities, resulting in more than 50 deaths and scores of injuries (Papke 1999). Gradually, the nation's military force wore down the strikers and by the end of the summer of 1894, the strike was broken, the Pullman Company reopened, and many workers returned to their jobs. The government prosecuted the union's leaders in criminal trials. Debs was convicted in November for violating the court injunction and sentenced to 6 months in federal prison.

This is the Chicago John Dewey came to in the summer of 1894. In June and July, in several letters to Alice, he described the turmoil in the city and his conversations with the strikers (Letter from John Dewey to Alice Chipman Dewey, June 30 and July 2, 1894, (00145); Letter from John Dewey to Alice Chipman Dewey, Frederick A., and Evelyn Dewey, July 14 and 16, 1894 (00159)). Dewey was wary of the labor troubles, which disrupted travel and delayed the mails. But he was deeply impressed by the strikers' commitment to a "common interest" and he followed the newspapers' daily reporting of the struggle. In early July, at the height of the dispute, Dewey wrote to Alice saying he thought the workers had little chance of success. But he viewed the strike as "a great thing & the beginning of greater" (Letter from John Dewey to Alice Chipman Dewey, June 30 and July 2, 1894, (00145)). In mid-July, Dewey wrote to Alice stating that the strike "has not only sobered . . . [the upper classes], but given the public mind an object lesson that it won't soon forget" (Letter from John Dewey to Alice Chipman Dewey, Frederick A., and Evelyn Dewey, July 14 and 16, 1894 (00159)). By the end of the conflict he was wholeheartedly behind the workers and formed a commitment to industrial democracy that would only strengthen with time (Westbrook 1992).

Turning to education, Chicago's dense urban population made the city a desirable location to establish new colleges and universities. Dewey was only one of many new professors moving to these new institutions. In addition to the recent founding of the University of Chicago, the Armour Institute of Technology began operations in 1890, North Park University opened its doors in 1891, and DePaul University was established in 1898. And, of interest to us, the Junior College Division in the University of Chicago was created in 1896. Although the 1890s was a period of growth for colleges and universities in Chicago, during this era the vast majority of students in school never went on to higher education (Dewey, *The School and Society*, 2008/1899). More than 50 percent of elementary school students dropped out before the end of the fifth grade. Only 5 percent of elementary students entered high school. Less than 1 percent of elementary students went on to enroll at a college or university.

Chicago was also the site of chronic poverty and harsh working conditions. The poor sanitation in tenement houses led to high mortality of infants, the infirm, and the elderly. Many immigrants and working poor labored in the city's slaughterhouses. These dangerous plants were often the site of horrible injuries and even death. Upton Sinclair described these conditions in his best-selling novel, *The Jungle* (1906).

Chicago also had a strong social reform movement, however, which was dedicated to improving the lives of the city's most unfortunate residents. Hull House, a settlement house founded by Jane Addams and Ellen Gates Starr, provided a temporary residence and community center for these Chicagoans (Elshtain 2002; Knight 2005, 2010). As Addams wrote, the settlement house was ". . . an experimental effort to aid in the solution of the social and industrial problems" generated "by the modern conditions of life in a great city" (Addams 1892, The Subjective Necessity for Social Settlements, published in Elshtain 2002, *The Jane Addams Reader*, p. 25). Because of his great respect for Addams and also his high regard for Hull House, Dewey became a trustee for the organization in 1897 and remained in this post until 1903. The philosopher and the social reformer developed a close and continuing relationship that lasted until Addams' death in 1935.

Addams would go on to win the Nobel Peace Prize in 1932, because of her decades-long efforts to bring an end to war. Dewey would go on to become the most respected philosopher in America. In 1894, however, both were working hard to make their mark in the world. Addams provided Dewey with a valuable perspective grounded on the real life experiences of immigrants and the working poor. What Dewey learned from Addams and also from his own experiences in Chicago was that an unregulated capitalist system in a large city had many adverse consequences that left the poor living in wretched living conditions.

In addition to his work at Hull House, where Dewey delivered an occasional lecture, the philosopher also immersed himself in many off-campus activities. He held classes at the Cook County Normal School. He visited the Art Institute and attended concerts in town with family and friends (Letter from John Dewey to Alice Chipman Dewey, October 14, 1894 (00209); Letter from John Dewey to Alice Chipman Dewey, October 19, 1894, Dewey (00211); Letter from John Dewey to Alice Chipman Dewey, November 1, 1894, Dewey (00218); Elshtain 2002). Dewey was not an isolated academic in Chicago. He ventured into the streets and was a keen observer of life off campus. Still, he would later regret not being even more engaged with his colleagues and the community.

Dewey's years in Chicago were also attended by personal loss. In the fall of 1894, Dewey left for Europe and traveled the continent with his family. Tragically, in circumstances that would be repeated almost 10 years later,

Dewey and his wife lost their 2 and a half year old son, Morris, to diphtheria in Milan in March 1895.

Over the next 10 years, Dewey maintained a busy schedule; teaching, writing, and traveling nationally and internationally to lecture. Dewey also established a Laboratory School associated with the University of Chicago, where he and his colleagues studied how children learn. Because Dewey had little experience in school administration, managing the Lab School became a burden (Dewey, *The School and Society*, 2008/1899, p. 57; Ryan 1995; Wirth 1966). Although the Lab School was important to Dewey, it was never embraced by Harper and this became a source of serious tension between the professor and the young president.

The New York years

The chronic struggles of the Lab School eventually discouraged Dewey and he resigned his faculty and administrative positions at Chicago in April 1904. Within 2 months, however, he had received and accepted an offer to join the Philosophy Department at Columbia University in New York (Ryan 1995). Dewey's departure from Chicago was bittersweet. On one hand, he had become deeply frustrated with President Harper and his lack of support for the Lab School. But the University of Chicago had provided Dewey with a stage, enabling him to become known as an accomplished philosopher and educator, both in the United States and abroad. Also, while in Chicago, Dewey had experiences that left him with vivid memories and a lifelong understanding of what life was like in a large industrial city. What Columbia offered him, however, was a stronger and more diverse philosophy department (Rockefeller 1991).

The move to New York was overshadowed, when on an intervening trip to Europe, family tragedy struck again. This time, Dewey's 8 year old son, Gordon, contracted typhoid and then, after a false recovery, died 6 weeks later in Ireland in September 1904 (Dykhuizen 1973; Ryan 1995). Dewey stayed in Europe and grieved with his family before leaving for the United States in January 1905. After returning home, Dewey devoted himself to his work. In the spring of 1905, he gave a series of well-received public lectures in New York. He was also elected to the presidency of the American Philosophical Association. Although Dewey had only been at Columbia for a few months, he quickly became everything that Columbia had sought in the new hire.

Over the next 5 years, Dewey continued to publish at an impressive rate and lectured at many universities including Harvard, Johns Hopkins, and the University of Illinois. In 1908, Dewey published *Ethics*, a philosophy textbook, with James H. Tufts. Tufts and Dewey had been colleagues at the University of Michigan and then at the University of Chicago (Stevenson 2008, "Introduction," MW#5). In 1910, Dewey published the first edition of *How We Think*. Both of these books were popular college texts. *Ethics* was often assigned reading in undergraduate philosophy courses (Stevenson 2008, "Introduction," MW#5). *How We Think* was used in teacher education courses (Ryan 1995).

Dewey's success attracted the attention of other universities. In 1906, the President at Stanford University, David Starr Jordan, inquired about Dewey's availability but then halted negotiations after the San Francisco earthquake wrecked the city and damaged parts of the Stanford campus (Hickman 2008, *Introduction to Correspondence Volume I*). In 1909, Dewey received inquiries from the University of California Berkeley. He declined to pursue this opportunity after the Trustees at Columbia granted him a significant raise. Feeling secure in his future at Columbia and happy with his environment, in July 1909 Dewey accepted an appointment as Head of Columbia's Philosophy Department (Hickman 2008, *Introduction to Correspondence Volume I*).

In 1910, Dewey's reputation as a scholar was enhanced again when he was elected to the National Academy of Sciences (Science 1910). This recognition came at a time, however, when his interests were diverging from the mainstream of American philosophy. In correspondence with a colleague, Dewey explained that philosophy was becoming a field marked by its increasing distance from real-life problems (Hickman 2008, *Introduction to Correspondence Volume I*; Letter from John Dewey to Henry Bawden, November 7, 1911, (02929)). It is not surprising, therefore, that Dewey began to look outside the university for experiences that resonated with his interest in reforming education and expanding democracy. For instance, he accepted leadership roles in organizations advocating for women's suffrage and civil rights for African Americans (Du Bois, *The Correspondence of W. E. B. Du Bois*, 1: 169; O'Donnell, "Suffragettes of Yesterday and Today," *Chicago Daily Tribune*, May 8, 1910). By 1910, and having reached the age of 51, Dewey had the stature that brought a new level of independence and he began to speak outside academia about many political issues (Ryan 1995).

Dewey's history of American education

From 1910 to 1920, Dewey focused much of his writing on the need to reform American education. In particular, he wrote extensively on industrial or vocational education and how schools tracked students into academic or vocational programs. In a series of essays and then in *Democracy and Education*, published in 1916, Dewey explained why schools and colleges needed to be reformed (Dewey 2008/1913, "Education from a Social Perspective," MW#7; Dewey 2008/1913, "Some Dangers in the Present Movement for Industrial Education," MW#7; Dewey 2008/1913, "Industrial Education and Democracy," MW#7; Dewey 2008/1913, "Should Michigan Have Vocational Education under 'Unit' or 'Dual' Control?" MW#7; Dewey 2008/1914, "A Policy of Industrial Education," MW#7; Dewey 2008/1915, "Industrial Education—A Wrong Kind," MW#8).

Dewey reminded his readers that during the colonial period, the overriding purpose of education was to provide the children of privilege with the capacity "of making their own way, of creating careers, of subduing nature" (Dewey 2008/1913, "Education from a Social Perspective MW#7," p. 115). Also, for many children, education provided an opportunity to develop the communication skills, interpersonal skills, and cultural capital needed to secure a high status social position in the church, politics, or business. Dewey noted that with the arrival of the industrial revolution, spurred on by scientific discoveries, an educational system focused on serving the privileged few was no longer sufficient.

In the United States and other Western nations, inventions such as the steam engine and the telegraph led to the mass production of goods, followed by their transportation to wholesalers who then disbursed them to retailers and then finally to customers. These new production, transportation, and communication networks required a well-trained workforce. Before the industrial revolution, children learned a vocation from older family members or through apprenticeships. By the late nineteenth century, however, school leaders recognized they needed to do much more and so they developed new industrial education programs in elementary and secondary schools. Dewey observed that these new curricula were changing schools in ways that were not always clearly understood. He identified three concerns.

First, this kind of dual track educational system replicated existing class divisions. Students destined for leadership in the community (the children of privilege), were well prepared in science, history, and the classics. These were the subjects necessary to prepare a student for a college education. Most elementary school students, however, were tracked into industrial education programs where the goal was to train them for manufacturing assembly lines without any real understanding of the context of their work. Of course, the life prospects for students going off to college and those going off to factory work were very different.

Second, dual track education in schools effectively limited the number of people prepared to make scientific discoveries. Under the existing education system, most of the students prepared for the business of inventing came from families living in homes with all the modern conveniences. In this kind of educational environment, there was little attention to the negative consequences of unregulated capitalism. Advancements in public health, public sanitation, food safety, safe housing, and safe manufacturing facilities were slow to arrive. These advancements were not a major focus of most colleges and universities because these were not a critical concern for most of the faculty or students. Improvements in these fields, therefore, were often triggered by outcries following human tragedies or from the negative publicity brought on by muckrakers.

Third, access to higher education was not based on competition and a bona fide assessment of academic merit. The students moving on to college were usually from wealthy families and gained admission through their social connections and ability to pay tuition. Dewey believed that a system that distributed higher education opportunities in this manner was fundamentally unfair. It also denied the nation the social benefits that would follow from educating a larger proportion of the population.

In short, Dewey argued, what was needed was a new "social perspective" to help reform education (Dewey 2008/1913, "Education from a Social Perspective MW#7."). Approaching education from a social perspective had two important implications. First, the purpose of education could no longer be to simply prepare students for assigned positions in "an established industrial structure" (Dewey 2008/1913, "Education from a Social Perspective MW#7," p. 127). Education from a social perspective required that educators examine industrial practice and the professions as they existed, and then, after determining the needs of the society, identify the changes needed to produce a stronger and more inclusive community. Second, approaching education from a social perspective required that educators help students learn that everyone has a responsibility to the society in which he lives. As Dewey wrote, a social perspective in education meant, "each person should devote himself to some work that contributes directly or indirectly to the enrichment of community interests, that enlarges the life of the group" (Dewey 2008/1913, "Education from a Social Perspective MW#7,"p. 126) It also meant that people should develop the capacity "of being useful to others through their work" (Dewey 2008/1913, "Education from a Social Perspective MW#7,"p. 126).

Dewey acknowledged that adopting a social perspective in education would mean more than adopting modest reforms in school operations. It would require, a "radical reconstruction of pedagogical principles" (Dewey 2008/1913, "Education from a Social Perspective MW#7," p. 127). But Dewey was convinced Americans had no real alternative. The traditional dualism that distinguished educational tracks for children based on wealth and family status was no longer viable in the modern world. He wrote,

the price that democratic societies will have to pay for their continuing health is the elimination of an oligarchy—the most exclusive and dangerous of all—that attempts to monopolize the benefits of intelligence and of the best methods for the profit of a few privileged ones, while practical labor, requiring less spiritual effort and less initiative, remains the lot of the great majority. (Dewey 2008/1913, "Education from a Social Perspective MW#7," p. 127)

Dewey was a forceful advocate for social change and he presented his arguments carefully and methodically. Consequently, he earned the respect of his academic peers across the country and around the world. He consistently distanced himself from revolutionary theories that advocated the violent overthrow of the American government. But he was convinced American society needed to change even if its political system did not. This change was needed not just to improve how children and adults learned. It was also necessary, he believed, in order to advance American democracy.

Dewey's view of America

Over the course of his career as a philosopher, educator, and public intellectual, Dewey published more than 40 books and hundreds of articles (Dykhuizen 1973). In the last decades of his life, he received honorary degrees from many universities and traveled extensively across the globe. Dewey was viewed by some as an agitator and was secretly surveilled by the Federal Bureau of Investigation. But he was regarded by many as the "conscience of the American people" (Commager 1950, p. 100).

The range of Dewey's life work was matched by the breadth and depth of his life experiences. He was married twice and a father to nine children, three of whom were adopted. In the course of Dewey's 92 years, American slaves were freed, women acquired the right to vote, 15 states were admitted to the Union, General Robert E. Lee surrendered at Appomattox Court House in Virginia, and the United States dropped atomic bombs on Nagasaki and Hiroshima. When Dewey died in 1952, the mild-mannered professor had lived a long life and left a mark across American society as a progressive. His writings on education, democracy, ethics, and experience have now been the subject of thousands of publications in many fields and disciplines (Boydston and Poulos 1978).

After his death, Dewey's reputation in America declined, although the causes of this development are not clear. This may have been the consequence of the nation's preoccupation with the emerging Cold War. Dewey's progressive politics were surely out of step with Senator Joe McCarthy and his followers, who went on a witch-hunt for Communist sympathizers in the government and also at colleges and universities. In any event, Dewey's reputation was not revived until 1979 when one of the nation's leading philosophers, Richard Rorty, asserted that along with Wittgenstein and Heidegger, Dewey was one of "the three most important philosophers of our century" (Rorty 1979, p. 5). Rorty's endorsement led to the reintroduction of Dewey across the humanities, the social sciences, and finally, in education.

John Dewey may appear to be an unusual figure to bring into a discussion of the values and priorities that might guide community colleges in the future. However, his writings make him especially relevant to the challenges facing these institutions. Almost 100 years ago, Dewey argued that everyone completing high school should have the opportunity to participate in adult education (Dewey 2008/1932, "Education and the Social Order," LW#9). He rejected the notion that the children of the wealthy should be tracked into a liberal arts program (delivered at the university) while the sons and daughters of the poor and working class were diverted into vocational curriculum (delivered at trade schools) (Dewey 2008/1916, "Democracy and Education," MW#9; Dewey 2008/1936, "Rationality in Education," LW#11). He advocated for an approach to education that respected the learner's experience. And he was not interested in leading all students to accept the "eternal truths" of the dominant culture as revealed in its "classics." For Dewey, the purpose of an education was to promote individual growth, to become a better person, and to acquire the skills and knowledge needed to work with others in building a better society. These beliefs are all central to the community college of today.

Additionally, Dewey regarded education as intimately connected to democracy. He understood that educational opportunity was an essential quality of a democracy. But the relationship between education and democracy went much farther than this. For Dewey, life in a democracy should be a constant process of identifying real problems, analyzing these problems in view of how they affect our lives, and then experimenting with solutions to solve them. For Dewey, therefore, a democracy required an educational system that is inclusive, focused on real problems, and dedicated to promoting the growth of the individual and the community.

Americans agree that their society should provide all adults with an opportunity to improve the quality of their life through education. It should also offer the opportunity to attain a comfortable station in life or, as we say, live the American Dream. But Dewey would tell us that a democracy should also provide students with much more than this. It should offer them the opportunity to develop the skills, dispositions, and values needed to contribute to their communities in meaningful ways. And, a democracy must continually identify the problems that hold people back, solve them, and then move forward.

Many community college faculty and staff view their work as central to the improvement of American democracy. But precisely how community college education and democracy are related is something we seldom get time to think about. In the chapters that follow, I highlight the values and priorities that have motivated community colleges throughout their history. I then show how Dewey's work provides the building blocks to construct a new and better normative vision for the community college of the future.

Conclusion

In this chapter I have provided a foundation for our encounter with Dewey in Chapters 8, 9, and 10. In these later chapters I say more about how he envisioned the relationship between education and democracy. What we will see there is that we can only begin to think about how educational institutions should be changed once we have an understanding of the kind of democracy we wish to live in and pass on to our children and grandchildren. Reforming educational institutions, without having a clear picture of the society we desire, may lead to measureable change in employment or economic growth but this will only be incremental change. If we wish to take the steps needed to make community colleges "Democracy's College," in more than a trivial way, we need a vision, a normative vision, that gets us moving beyond access, beyond completion, and on to the kind of educational culture that will promote individual growth and the development of democratic communities. And, as I argue, for those who see community colleges as having a central role in the development of American democracy, Dewey is a person who can help point us in the right direction.

PART TWO

The evolution of the community college

4

The junior college movement

Introduction

Any attempt to propose a new normative vision for the community college needs to account for the institution's past. The community college's roots extend back to the early 1900s and its institutional predecessor, the junior college. In this chapter, I begin by describing the nation's first junior college programs, established in Chicago and nearby Joliet. I then turn to California to explain how junior college programs began in that state. The record indicates that senior university leaders in Illinois and California were powerful advocates for the development of junior college programs. Their efforts were complemented by the hard work of public school leaders. All of these leaders viewed junior college programs as a vital component in the education continuum. But they viewed junior college programs as most effective when they were part of the public high school or in some cases as a part of the university. University and public school leaders agreed, however, that the overriding purposes of junior college programs were (a) to preserve the integrity of the universities by relieving them from increasing political pressure to admit more students and (b) to strengthen public high school curricula by offering coursework students would need to gain admission to the university. Next, I provide a brief account of the work of early junior college researchers. These researchers found that junior college programs were an important innovation not because of the curricula they offered or the educational outcomes they achieved. Instead they were important because of the work they did in serving other institutions or accommodating the needs of parents and the community.

These findings should not be surprising. In the Midwest and the West, junior college programs, and then later, standalone junior colleges, entered an environment already dominated by public schools, on one hand, and 4-year colleges and universities on the other. Junior college programs survived because their leaders understood that their success required the cooperation of other institutions in the education continuum. Their leaders also understood they needed to accommodate the interests of parents and other community leaders. Satisfying student educational needs was certainly a priority. But it was not the most important priority.

The Chicago junior colleges

Most historians in the field report that junior college education began in Chicago and nearby Joliet in the 1890s and early 1900s. In 1896, the private University of Chicago began to offer junior college courses. In Joliet in 1902, the city's public high school began to offer its own slate of junior college courses. In both cases, the objective was *not* to establish a new institution but to deliver courses to help students make the transition from high school to the university. In both cases, the courses offered were aligned with an already existing college or high school curriculum. These new junior college courses were an important educational innovation. We need to acknowledge the innovative leaders that developed them. But these classes were also shaped by the needs of new universities and high schools operating in and around Chicago.

As I mentioned earlier, at the turn of the twentieth century, Chicago was a city undergoing great social change. Upton Sinclair's *The Jungle* accurately portrayed an urban society distinguished by its racial and ethnic diversity, a large immigrant population, income inequality, stark poverty, poor housing, and dangerous work conditions. In 1900, with a population of 1.7 million, Chicago was the second largest city in the United States (United States Census Office 1901, Volume 1). And, although approximately 525,000 Chicago residents were of school age (5 to 20 years old) only 250,000 were enrolled in school (United States Census Office 1901, Volume 2, Chapter 7, Table 49, p. 386). Eighty-five percent of these students were enrolled at elementary schools. This distribution in the schools reflected two important facts of life in many early twentieth century American cities. First, the extensive poverty and lack of child labor laws forced many children to leave school after completing their elementary grades to work in factories. Second, although elementary schools were common throughout the nation, high schools were far fewer in number.

Despite the low high school enrollments, the city's rapid population growth justified the creation of new higher education institutions such as the University of Chicago. The university's president, William Raney Harper, envisioned an educational system that had two very different objectives. First, he openly recruited the best faculty in the nation to staff a new elite university. He then encouraged these professors to enroll the most promising students available. Second, Harper wanted to develop an educational system that integrated and coordinated high school, college, and university curricula (Mayer 1957; Storr 1966). Only this kind of educational system would satisfy Harper's driving ambition to "educate everyone everywhere" (Mayer 1957, p. 52). Under Harper's plan, after students completed high school they would take general education courses and this "junior college" curriculum would prepare them for university study. The junior college curriculum would help ensure that the university had a steady stream of qualified students prepared for the more demanding university courses. But for Harper and his faculty, the junior college curriculum was also an important "clearing-house system" that weeded out students not ready for the university (Storr 1966, p. 120). A clearing-house system was essential if Harper's professors and teachers were going to simultaneously "educate everyone everywhere" while also maintaining academic standards in its university courses.

In the more established and heavily populated Northeast, universities relied upon a well-organized private academy system to sustain enrollments and filter out secondary students who demonstrated little aptitude for university work. But in the hurly-burly Midwest, where the quality of newly established public high schools was suspect, Harper's junior college program accomplished two objectives. It helped the University of Chicago develop and maintain adequate enrollment while also establishing an effective filtering system.

In the case of the Joliet High School, delivery of junior college courses evolved under different circumstances. In 1901, the Township of Joilet opened a new state-of-the-art high school that was the pride of the community (Brown 1901). The new building had 87 rooms and was designed to accommodate 1,400 students. It included the most recent innovations in teaching laboratories and classrooms. The new high school was also constructed with the best materials available. The hall floors and stairs were made of Vermont white marble and trimmed with Tennessee black marble.

The Principal of the high school, J. Stanley Brown, was a driving force in getting the new facility built. But his decision to deliver a junior college program was due, in large measure, to the influence of William Raney Harper. Harper and Brown were both Baptists and would regularly discuss education while away at Baptist conventions (Eells 1931). Harper told Brown that a junior college program at Joliet High School would appeal to the state's universities just as his own junior college program had secured the support of his faculty at the University of Chicago. Such a program, therefore, would help Joliet High School graduates gain admission at the increasingly selective state universities. Harper's prediction would prove to be true.

In 1901, at the dedication of the new high school building, the president of the University of Illinois, Andrew S. Draper, spoke to the assembled guests and praised them for their accomplishment (Haggard 1930). Draper commended the people of Joliet for building a handsome new facility. It would certainly provide the city's recent high school graduates with a new opportunity for study. For Draper, however, the development of a junior college program at the new high school was another indicator of Joilet's progressive spirit. Students completing the high school's junior college program would require less tutoring and academic support at the university. Consequently, the cost of educating them would be less as well.

Principal Brown explained that the new junior college courses would benefit high school students and their parents in other ways too. First, they would allow students "to be under the influence of the home during later adolescence" (Haggard 1930, p. 433). Second, they would provide, for those interested, "occupational training of college grade" (Haggard 1930, p. 433). Finally, the delivery of lower division college courses at Joliet High School provided an educational opportunity for students, "financially unable to go away to college or university" (Haggard 1930, p. 433). For Brown, the new junior college courses had many advantages that had little to do with limiting the university's costs.

Illinois' experiment with junior college programs continued after Joliet and the University of Chicago. But the expansion of public programs was gradual. Twenty-eight years later, in 1929, the state had only 12 public junior college programs and public school districts operated each of these programs. Twelve private junior college programs were also operating at this time. The state legislature did not pass legislation authorizing independent public junior colleges until 1931 (Krebs, Katsinas and Johnson 1999). Legislation providing state funding for public junior colleges was not enacted until 1943.

The record regarding the development of junior colleges in Chicago and Illinois is revealing. The first junior colleges were established to strengthen other educational institutions—a private university and a public high school. Both junior college programs had the strong support of university leaders who regarded the new courses as an important device to prepare or screen out students intending to study at the university. Finally, even though Illinois was home to the nation's first junior college programs, once the needs of area universities and high schools were met, the state was slow to authorize their independent operation and even slower to fund them. To be sure, the delivery of junior college courses was an important educational innovation in the state. Private institutions helped meet the demand for these courses. But the expansion of state-subsidized junior college programs did not occur quickly. After public junior college programs began operating in Illinois, it took the state almost 40 years to formally institutionalize them and place them on an independent financial foundation.

The California junior colleges

The nation's first junior college courses were offered by a university and high school located in Illinois. But the first state legislation authorizing the delivery of junior college courses was enacted in California in 1907. Again, university leaders were strong proponents of this development (Eells 1931). The most visible leader in the effort to establish junior college programs was Dr Alexis Lange, a professor of English at the University of California and then later, the dean of the University's School of Education. Lange consistently advocated for the creation of these programs in conversations with state legislators and he was supported by the President of Stanford University, Dr David Starr Jordan. Both Lange and Jordan argued that junior college courses were needed to protect their universities from enrollment pressures emerging in a large state whose population was growing quickly.

The 1907 California law authorized the governing board of any public school district to offer courses similar to those found in the first 2 years of a university curriculum. But it did not require that any high school deliver junior college courses. It did not authorize the establishment of new educational institutions. It merely permitted high schools to offer these courses. As one researcher reported, it only authorized the "upward extension" of the public high school (Eells 1931, p. 89).

In what was a surprise to several observers, the 1907 legislation had no immediate impact (Cooper 1928; Eells 1931). Given the authority to proceed, no school district offered a new junior college curriculum. It would be another 3 years before a school district took advantage of the law and scheduled a slate of junior college courses. The first to do this was the Fresno High School and it enrolled 15 students in its new junior college curriculum in 1910 (Eells 1931). Interest in the new junior college courses did grow gradually, however, and by 1917 an additional 15 public high schools were offering junior college courses.

The 1907 law opened the door to junior college education in California. But it had an important limitation (Eells 1931). It did not create a funding mechanism to support these courses. This problem was readily apparent to educators and lawmakers. But it was not addressed until 1917. Then, legislation was enacted authorizing public high schools to establish junior college departments. Courses offered by junior college departments could be supported by state and local tax revenues in the same manner as courses offered by other high school departments. This dedicated funding stream prepared the way for a significant expansion in junior college course offerings and enrollments. But the United States' entry into World War I in April 1917 led thousands of young Californians to enlist in the Army and Navy. Soon six high schools were forced to cancel their junior college programs because of low enrollment.

When the war ended in November 1918, the veterans returned home and many chose to go to college. It would be another 3 years, however, before California legislators revisited the status of the state's junior college programs. Then in 1921, the legislature authorized the establishment of new independent public junior college districts. The creation of a junior college district required: (a) a positive vote of the proposed district's residents, (b) approval by the state board of education, (c) a minimum assessed value of real estate in the district to support local taxes, and (d) a minimum high school enrollment. For the first time in California, independent junior college districts were authorized to open a junior college and fund it with state and local revenue. The first institution established under the 1921 law was Modesto Junior College, which offered its first classes in September 1922 (Eells 1931).

The 1921 law was another step forward in the junior college movement. But it was not a radical innovation. The law did not affect the existing junior college departments operating at public high schools. More importantly, the law came with new additional requirements that regulated the operation of junior colleges. The law required that state university faculty inspect and accredit junior college courses. It also required that state university faculty establish the qualifications for junior college instructors. As a practical matter, this arrangement helped ensure that students taking courses at a junior college would receive university credit when they transferred. But the academic autonomy of junior colleges was clearly limited. As one scholar later noted, during this era the California junior college was sometimes little more than "a bookkeeping and financial transaction" between a high school and a university (Clark 1960b, p. 12).

Eight years later, in 1929, the California General Assembly responded to taxpayer concerns and placed a brake on junior college expansion. The 1929 law limited the creation of additional junior college districts by imposing higher minimum real estate valuations for proposed districts and higher minimum high school enrollments. Junior college advocates openly criticized the law and viewed it as regressive (Eells 1931).

Even with this cautious and haphazard beginning, however, by 1930 California had become the center of the junior college movement in America. And, it would retain this leadership position for the next 80 years. In 1930, junior college courses were being offered at 35 public institutions in the state. Fourteen private institutions were also offering junior college courses (Eells 1931). Ten years later, the number of public institutions had increased to 48 and the number of privates to 16 (Eells 1941). Accordingly, by 1940, the junior college had become an established part of the state's subsidized higher education system and the future for California and the nation was clear. The growth, going forward, would be in the public sector.

As new junior college programs were established across the nation, education researchers tried to gauge the direction and momentum of the movement. Some produced reports for federal and state government agencies. Others published in scholarly journals or spoke at state and national education conferences. Each was a strong advocate for the movement. And each produced a picture of the movement that was generally consistent with what happened in Illinois and California.

Floyd Marion McDowell

In 1919, Floyd Marion McDowell completed a 140-page report on the junior college for the Bureau of Education in the United States Department of the Interior. McDowell collected data from scholarly papers, professional journals, government reports, and newspaper articles (McDowell 1919). He also interviewed or surveyed high school principals, state education officials, junior college administrators, and university faculty. McDowell's report was the first major attempt to present a national picture of the junior college movement.

McDowell found that across the country, the earliest advocates for junior college education were senior leaders at American universities. In 1852 Henry P. Tappan, President of the University of Michigan, argued that the first 2 years of university coursework should be transferred to the secondary schools. William Watts Folwell, President of the University of Minnesota, suggested the same in 1875. And McDowell found, as I have already described, that university leaders in Illinois and California were early advocates for junior college programs in those states.

McDowell's account of the junior college movement placed these new programs in a broad educational context. He found that nationwide, four different educational institutions had been instrumental in developing junior college programs: the university, the normal school (teacher training schools), the high school, and the private liberal arts college. Each institution had its own organizational reasons for supporting the creation of junior college programs.

University leaders advocated for such programs, usually located at public high schools, because they relieved their institutions from increasing political pressure to admit more students. Junior college programs also served as a clearinghouse that could divert unprepared students away from university study. And junior college programs that included vocational curricula accomplished this diversionary function while also providing students with an alternative career path.

Normal schools also advocated for the development of junior college programs but for very different reasons. Normal schools grew in substantial numbers during the last half of the nineteenth century as states worked to produce the teachers needed in new and expanding elementary and secondary schools. Because teaching was a low status occupation, normal schools were also low in the higher education hierarchy, subordinate to universities and private liberal arts colleges. In fact, normal school graduates usually did not earn a degree. Instead, they were only awarded a certificate or a diploma certifying their competency to teach certain grades or subjects. Normal school leaders backed the junior college movement because they wanted to incorporate these programs into their curriculum, provide their students with a pathway to the university, and as a result, acquire higher standing in the education hierarchy.

Public schools also had an organizational interest in developing junior college programs. As I noted earlier, university leaders argued that the first 2 years of college coursework were more closely related to secondary education than university education. Public school officials were eager to show that this assessment was correct and that they could pick up this new responsibility. Consequently, the development of junior college programs at public high schools brought them higher status in the education hierarchy.

For McDowell, a fourth influence was the private liberal arts college. During the first decades of the twentieth century, increasing state regulation placed new administrative pressures on these small private colleges. They were required to report their financial affairs in a more regular and systematic manner and this posed significant challenges for institutions often working with a small staff and struggling to meet the payroll. Also, liberal arts colleges were now under greater market pressure because larger state universities were expanding their student enrollments. For many liberal arts colleges, therefore, enrollment growth and financial stability were best achieved by converting to junior college status. This conversion let the colleges limit their course offerings to the first 2 years of a traditional undergraduate program. Also, inexpensive part-time instructors could teach junior college courses. This practice would become a signature feature of the junior college.

In addition to these institutional considerations, McDowell identified other factors offered to justify the creation of junior college programs. In a survey of public junior college leaders, he found the most frequent reason offered to explain the establishment of a program was the, "desire of parents to keep children at home" (McDowell 1919, p. 28). And the most frequent reason given by the leaders of private junior colleges was "to provide opportunities for higher education under church control" (McDowell 1919, p. 36).

McDowell's 1919 report affirmed that in the first two decades of the twentieth century, the junior college movement was alive and well. What the report also revealed, however, was that there were significant institutional and social forces fueling the movement. Universities, high schools, normal schools, and private liberal arts colleges all had institutional reasons to support the movement. The creation of junior college curricula helped institutions avoid enrollment pressures (the university), enhance their stature (the high school and the normal school), or secure their future in an increasingly competitive market (the liberal arts college). Also, both parents and church leaders had an interest in offering programs that secured their influence over students. To be sure, serving the educational needs and interests of students was a priority. But this was not the highest high priority for leaders preoccupied with their own institution's survival.

George F. Zook

Another early researcher reporting on the junior college movement was George F. Zook (Buddy 1990). In 1922, Zook was Chief of the Higher Education Division at the US Bureau of Education. Zook would go on to be the President of the University of Akron (1925–33), the Commissioner of Education for President Franklin D. Roosevelt (1933–34), and then the chief executive of the American Council on Education (1934–50). While serving as the president of the American Council on Education (ACE), Zook was asked by President Harry Truman in 1946 to chair the President's Commission on Higher Education. Throughout Zook's career he was a strong advocate for junior college education. In the 1920s, however, one of Zook's primary interests was explaining the emergence of the junior college.

In a 1922 journal article, Zook, a historian by trade, reminded his readers that in the United States, the elementary and higher education systems developed simultaneously in the seventeenth century (Zook 1922). Secondary education—in the United States, the high school—was not established until the nineteenth century. He observed that this uneven development reflected a lack of consensus on how American children should be educated. Zook found that the early elementary schools were organized and funded by towns and then later the state. They provided young children with a basic education enabling them to read and write. However, colleges, established by churches and wealthy benefactors, typically limited enrollment to the children of privilege and provided them with the liberal education deemed necessary for attaining leadership positions in the community, the church, and the state.

Secondary schools, the link between elementary education and higher education, and the mechanism that opened up higher education to a wider segment of the population, were not developed in most American towns until the late nineteenth century. Zook claimed that the initial role of junior college programs was to strengthen secondary schools and improve the pathway to higher education. And, he argued, several considerations confirmed the wisdom in developing these programs. First, the six-year period spanning the high school grades and the junior college years mapped neatly on to the normal period of adolescence. Second, an additional 2 years of secondary education provided the knowledge base needed by students entering professional schools (e.g., law and medicine). Third, universities were spending too much to teach lower division courses—work that was best handled in less-expensive junior college programs. Fourth, junior college education gave students an opportunity for further study without requiring that they leave home. Fifth and finally, Zook argued that the dominant motivation for the junior-college movement was "economy in education," which for him meant using junior college courses to improve alignment between high schools on one hand and universities and professional schools on the other (Zook 1922, p. 578). Better alignment would decrease the period of time students were in school and ensure they would not need to repeat courses once they were admitted to a university or professional school.

Zook recognized that junior college programs were also growing because of the increasing demand for higher education. Indeed, student enrollments were growing across the education continuum. State compulsory education laws were keeping more students in school and more of them developed an aptitude for further study. An increasingly complex economy also created a need for further education. But, like McDowell, he observed that the junior college movement was largely driven by the needs and interests of other institutions, and in particular, the high school and the university.

Looking forward, Zook identified a new consideration beginning to play an important role in the junior college movement. Junior college education, he argued, was now a priority for the states. The states needed successful junior college programs for the same reasons they needed successful public schools and universities. A well-educated citizenry was necessary if the nation was to achieve greater economic prosperity, a richer culture, and a sounder democracy. To be sure, achieving these ends would require a greater "concentration of educational authority in the state" (Zook 1922, p. 581). And, he wrote, the public must be "prepared to spend more for secondary and higher education than ever before" (Zook 1922, p. 583). But, he believed, the public benefits of education would justify these changes.

Leonard V. Koos

In 1925, Leonard V. Koos, a professor at the University of Chicago, published a comprehensive work on the junior college, describing its evolution since the turn of the century. Koos was a former public school superintendent and another strong junior college advocate (Koos 1925). His book, *The Junior-College Movement*, became a hallmark of early junior college research and a guide for junior college practitioners. It presented and explained findings he had published in a two-volume technical work the preceding year and it outlined themes he would revisit for decades. Koos collected data for this research through (a) an examination of course listings in junior college catalogs, (b) surveys of the parents of junior college students, (c) surveys of high school and junior college administrators, (d) campus visits to junior colleges, and (e) an examination of the literature on junior colleges (Koos 1925).

Koos found that the junior college programs of the early 1920s had four predominant purposes. The first was "the Isthmian Function" which was the delivery of the first 2 years of college coursework for students intending to transfer to a university. Koos agreed with other researchers that the subjects and pedagogy of the first 2 years of a university education were more closely aligned to the subjects and pedagogy found at high school. It made sense academically, therefore, to fulfill the Isthmian Function in high school-based junior college programs.

The second purpose was to provide students, not intending to enroll at the university, with an opportunity to acquire the skills and knowledge needed to accomplish other objectives. In some cases students would take courses to prepare for a career, such as those in business or the allied health fields (e.g., nursing, pharmacy). In other cases, however, students might take general education courses to "round out" their education. Koos referred to this purpose as "democratizing educational opportunities," which meant that a junior college education could serve a wide range of student interests (Koos 1930, p. 13).

The third purpose of junior college education was to provide a "conserving and socializing" influence over students (Koos 1925, p. 166). Here Koos was identifying a purpose that had been noted by McDowell. Both researchers had found that parents and teachers viewed high school graduates as children who still required supervision. The advantage of junior college programs, therefore, was that students could live at home and still take college courses. Koos and McDowell were also noting a historical fact sometimes overlooked today. That is, in the early twentieth century, when the legal age of majority was 21, most junior college students were identified, legally and culturally, as children.

For Koos, the junior college's fourth purpose was to facilitate the reorganization of higher education. Koos and many of his colleagues regarded the existing education hierarchy as confusing and ineffective. The transition from elementary schools to high schools had been awkward and only improved by the development of the intermediary junior high school, beginning in the mid- to late nineteenth century. In the early twentieth century, the transition from high school to higher education was also clumsy, with students often entering the university unprepared. Koos believed that a reorganization of education to more tightly align secondary education with higher education was essential and he considered junior college programs as key to accomplishing this goal. Koos believed that the most logical way to reorganize public education was to impose a new 6-4-4 plan (Koos 1925). The plan called for a 6-year elementary school, a 4-year secondary school, and a 4-year postsecondary school, ending with a 2-year junior college program. Koos' plan was a more educationally robust 14-year alternative to the predominant 6-2-4 structure which only provided students with 12 years of education.

Koos was a prolific researcher and published more than 25 journal articles on junior college education during the 1920s, 1930s, and 1940s. He wrote on a wide range of subjects. But two themes were consistent throughout his work. The first was his belief that junior college education should be a part of the high school. The second was that junior college programs could significantly improve an educational system that had serious shortcomings. Koos believed that this system let students leave the beneficial structure of the high school too early. It also graduated students unprepared for university coursework. Adding a junior college program to the public school system would solve this problem, which, at its core, was a problem of administration and organization.

Walter Eells

In 1931, Walter Eells, another junior college advocate and a professor of education at Stanford University, published *The Junior College*, a book intended for use in graduate education courses (Eells 1931). Eells collected his data from (a) government reports, (b) institutional reports, (c) research journals, and (d) personal communications with education officials and researchers. Like McDowell, Zook, and Koos, Eells also tried to offer a meaningful description of the movement and for him the most important general distinction for junior colleges was their status as either public or private (Eells 1931). He identified four types of public junior colleges: (a) the branch campus of a state university, (b) the two-year standalone state college, (c) the district college, and (d) the city college. Within the private group, Eells identified these types: (a) the branch campus of a private university, (b) the denominational college, (c) the special type college (e.g., the YMCA junior colleges), and (d) the proprietary college.

Eells also identified four primary functions transcending both public and private junior colleges. The four functions were: (a) the popularizing function,

(b) the preparatory function, (c) the terminal function, and, (d) the guidance function. By the term "popularizing function" Eells referred to the delivery of college level courses to a new and wider range of students. Eells believed that this function was still evolving as junior colleges were also experimenting with the delivery of lectures, public debates, and plays to students and community residents.

The second function Eells identified was the preparatory function and junior colleges did this work when they prepared students for university study. Eells noted that across the country, this was the most common work carried out by these programs. Indeed, he observed, 90 percent of California's junior college students intended to transfer to the university or some other higher education institution. But, in his view, many junior college programs were falling down in this work. Junior colleges were often limited "by inferior facilities in the way of library, laboratories, etc." (Eells 1931, p, 278). Consequently, they often failed to adequately prepare students for the university. As Eells reluctantly observed, there were "many weak and inefficient" colleges engaged in the business of transfer education (Eells 1931, p. 280). And many university administrators had come to look upon junior college graduates with "doubt and skepticism" (Eells 1931,p. 280).

The terminal function referred to the delivery of 2-year technical programs that prepared students for employment. Students enrolled in these programs were developing the skills needed to hold jobs in fields such as law enforcement, retail sales, engineering, and also allied health (e.g., nursing, pharmacy, and optometry). There were far fewer students enrolled in these technical programs when compared to those in the transfer programs. But junior college leaders believed these curricula would distinguish the junior college of the future from other institutions. Eells was among these leaders and he viewed terminal education as the future of junior college education.

The fourth function Eells identified was the guidance function. He viewed this as the foundation for the other three. In other words, junior college programs would only succeed in providing greater educational opportunities, a sound preparatory curriculum, and high quality terminal education if students were properly advised and guided to the programs that best fit their needs and abilities. Students who were well served in this manner would be sorted into the right programs.

Eells' discussion of the public - private distinction and the different junior college functions was not unique. Others had addressed both topics. But his writing anticipated the growing importance of these topics in ways that others did not. Over the next 80 years, the public - private distinction would become critically important if only because almost all of the nation's community colleges would become publicly governed and publicly subsidized. Also, Eells' attention to junior college *educational* functions exceeded that given by earlier researchers and he unambiguously prioritized student needs as key to describing the institution. Accommodating the institutional needs of universities and high schools would remain a priority. For Eells, however, the most important aspect of junior college education was meeting student needs.

Conclusion

The first fruit of the junior college movement appeared in Illinois and California as a consequence of the strong advocacy of university administrators and public school leaders. In Illinois, junior college programs were promoted by powerful university administrators and served the institutional interests of both universities and high schools. Gradually, junior college programs at the high schools grew in number and after several decades were accorded independent status and local and state revenue streams. In California, where the historical record is better than that found in most states, the progress of the junior college movement was positive but erratic. The processes for organizing and funding of junior college programs changed often. Junior college programs opened and then closed because of low enrollment. Junior college courses were often the product of high school and university negotiations. And the available data indicate that many junior college programs had poor facilities and questionable records of success in preparing students for transfer. But high schools gained prestige in the community from having a junior college program. California's universities were able to refer high school graduates to a junior college program when they did not appear ready for the academic challenge.

Publications by McDowell, Zook, Koos, and Eells provide a broader but consistent picture of the junior college movement in the first three decades of the twentieth century. These researchers described the diversity of the movement and the diversity of junior college programs. They also identified a wide range of purposes or functions that were offered to justify the delivery of junior college education. When we step back from these different works we see that the stated purposes of junior college education included everything from securing parental supervision of students to offering vocational education to facilitating a reorganization of American education. These early researchers also discerned the distinct roles of other educational institutions in promoting junior college education. During the early years, the establishment and operation of junior college programs was used to advance the interests of high schools, normal schools, private liberal arts colleges and universities.

The conventional history of community colleges recalls the junior college movement as one defined by steady growth in student enrollments and the number of institutions in operation. And this account of the junior college movement is true. However, it is also incomplete. What a closer examination of the record reveals is that in the early years, the overarching priority of the junior college movement was simply institutional survival in an environment that had yet to provide stable governing and funding processes. Junior college leaders understood this; they accurately identified the institutional, political, economic, and cultural forces that had control over their future; and they reached accords with them. Consequently, the values that ensured this survival were flexibility, efficiency, accommodation, and service to other institutions. This chameleon identity should not be regarded as a deficiency. It was simply the path to survival. Of course, educating students was an important priority. Junior college leaders recognized that their programs offered life-changing opportunities that never would have existed without them. But the significant demands placed upon the junior colleges did not come from students, legally and culturally, the children of the community. They came from educational leaders, politicians, and policymakers who were still trying to determine what the junior college was and what it should be in the decades ahead.

5

The Great Depression and the junior college

Introduction

During the 1930s, the evolution of junior college education continued on a track of growth. Throughout the decade, as had happened in the past, universities and high schools played a major role in guiding their evolution. But, as more junior college programs achieved independent status, their future was also shaped by the emergence of the adult education movement, the struggles of private liberal arts colleges, the increasing role of the federal government in education and a new focus on older students, that is, adult learners. Most importantly, the evolution of junior colleges was influenced by the Great Depression and the federal government's response. Two developments, in particular, foreshadowed the future of community colleges. One was the federal government's decision to use public 2-year institutions as a vehicle to carry out national economic policy. This was reflected in the creation of emergency junior colleges during the Great Depression. The second was the creation of a student financial aid. This new program, beyond the capacity or at least the interests of many state governments, revealed how the federal government could have a great impact on junior college education without opening a building or hiring an instructor. In this chapter I examine each of these influences and explain their significance.

The adult education movement

During the 1920s and 1930s, researchers and government officials like Zook, Koos, and Eells provided important support for the junior college movement. During this same era, however, the nation saw an explosion of adult education programs. The increasing popularity of adult education was reflected in the establishment of the American Association for Adult Education (AAAE) in 1926. The AAAE was founded by intellectuals and adult educators and it received significant financial support from the Carnegie Foundation (Day 1981). Its formal purpose was to collect and disseminate information on adult education and also to support research on adult education issues. More informally, however, the AAAE became the organization that took on the responsibility of convincing the nation that "adult education is a new educational frontier, a new educational challenge" (Day 1981, p. 3).

The offices of the AAAE were located in New York, which had become a hub of adult education. New adult education programs were established, both in the city's higher education institutions and in its community organizations. In 1929, AAAE began publication of the quarterly *Journal of Adult Education* (JAE), which became the voice of the organization. Contributors to the JAE wrote on a wide range of issues and this reflected the fact that adult education programs were being offered by libraries, lyceums, Chautauquas, men's and women's clubs, museums, radio stations, theaters, prisons, corporations, religious organizations, settlement houses, labor unions, teacher colleges, university extension offices, college and university alumni associations, and public schools (Ely 1948; Rowden 1934, 1936). At its core, the adult education movement was inclusive and had the active support and participation of educators but also many outside the education establishment such as philanthropists, newspaper editors, religious leaders, civic officials, corporate officers, and labor leaders (Day 1981).

What the adult education movement lacked, however, was a set of institutionalized funding mechanisms comparable to those supporting public schools and many public junior colleges. This lack of dedicated funding streams was due, in part, to the independent and open-minded spirit that motivated the movement. It was also due, however, to the movement's prioritization of learning over courses and credentials, the traditional institutional markers that have served as a vehicle and justification for funding.

The adult education movement grew, however, even during the difficult 1930s because innovative educators were able to identify specific adult education needs and then bring together the instructors, funding sources, facilities, and students needed to run programs. What these educators did not do, however, was seek out a permanent relationship with state and local governments. And, given the ethos of the movement, this was no surprise. By the end of the 1930s, however, the adult education movement was losing some of its energy. The JAE ceased publication in 1941. Adult education programs would continue to be offered by a wide range of providers both during and after World War II. But the unique blend of optimism, idealism, and spontaneity that had invigorated the movement in the 1920s and 1930s was left behind.

During the late 1930s, junior college leaders noted the direction of the adult education movement and they made the bargain that adult education leaders did not. They retained their institutional ties to public schools and universities even as they strove for independent status. They accepted the state regulation that was required in order to secure government funding. In other words, junior college leaders worked hard to find a place for their institutions in the formal American education hierarchy. They bet that institutionalization and regulation were the most promising paths to growth and greater stability and they were right.

The private liberal arts college

During the 1920s and 1930s, the private liberal arts college faced serious challenges as a result of several factors. First, during the 1920s, significant enrollment growth at state universities and public junior colleges placed increasing market pressure on private liberal arts colleges. The enrollment growth at public colleges and universities was problematic for private liberal arts colleges because it provided tangible evidence of the need for higher state appropriations to these institutions. These new revenues, in turn, were used to expand and improve the public campuses, thus posing even stiffer competition for the liberal arts colleges. Second, with the onset of the Great Depression, many students could not afford the relatively high tuition charged by liberal arts colleges and, as a consequence, enrollments at these institutions declined from approximately 570,000 students in 1929 to 500,000 in 1933 (Snyder 1993). This decrease in enrollment and tuition revenue placed great strain on the institution that had dominated American higher education for three centuries. Third, the financial losses incurred as a result of the Great Depression reduced the value of institutional endowments and also the size of gifts and bequests given by benefactors and alumni (Cutten 1939). These losses hit private liberal arts colleges especially hard and their leaders were forced to make adjustments in program and course offerings.

Presidents at the liberal arts colleges acknowledged the dire circumstances confronting their institutions. For example, in 1930, Homer Rainey, the president at Franklin College, a small liberal arts college in Indiana observed that, "the traditional liberal-arts college is caught between the upper and the nether millstones" (Rainey 1930, p. 381). Of course, Rainey was referring to the expanding capacity at state universities and the growth in the number of public junior colleges. He predicted that private liberal arts colleges would recover and prevail against their competition and he cited three reasons to explain why the public junior college could not be regarded as a long-term threat.

First, Rainey contended, most local governments lacked the resources needed to establish and operate a junior college. Indeed, Rainey believed that no more than 300 cities could afford to take on this responsibility. Consequently, he concluded, "it takes only a limited understanding to appreciate the fact that the junior college will never become a universal system in the United States" (Rainey 1930, p. 383). Second, Rainey maintained that the growth of junior colleges would be limited by what he viewed as their inability to deliver quality education. As he explained,

> The fact is that many of the public junior colleges now in existence are little more than glorified high schools. . . . The training of the faculty will not compare at all favorably with that of the liberal-arts colleges. The average salary for teachers in these institutions is considerably lower than that of the independent liberal-arts colleges, and the absence of library and laboratory facilities is marked. (Rainey 1930, p. 384)

Third, Rainey also saw the emerging vocational education focus of junior colleges as an area of growth but one that would ultimately consign these institutions to marginal status in the American education hierarchy. He told his readers,

> probably the field where the junior college will serve best in the future will be in providing adult vocational training in night schools to those already gainfully employed, and this type of vocational training will most likely be limited to training in trade courses and for clerks, bookkeepers, and stenographers. (Rainey 1930, p. 384)

Rainey was both right and wrong about the future of junior colleges. He was right in predicting that junior colleges would expand their vocational mission. But he was wrong in predicting that their growth would be limited. And he was blind to a reality that many others plainly saw. The growing importance of vocational education would help junior colleges garner the long-term support of state and federal governments.

In any event, the 1930s were a period of serious turmoil for private liberal arts colleges and their struggles often worked to the advantage of public junior colleges. Of course, behind the fall and rise of both institutions was a much larger factor and this was the Great Depression.

The Great Depression

To put the Great Depression in perspective, a few details are needed (Kennedy 1999; Schlesinger 1987; Vangiesen and Schwenk 2001). The stock market crash of October 29, 1929 led to the drastic reduction of capital available for investment, lending, and business expansion and this led to the contraction and then collapse of many businesses. As workers lost their jobs, consumption fell and businesses laid off employees to limit their expenditures. The consequence was that economic productivity fell precipitously. For example, in the United States the Gross National Product (GNP) fell by approximately 50 percent from 1929 to 1933 and this was accompanied by a significant increase in unemployment. Before the crash in 1929, unemployment had been at 3.3 percent. This rose to 8.9 percent in 1930 and then up to 15.9 percent in 1931. The rise continued through 1932 when it reached 23.6 percent and then it finally peaked in 1933 at 24.9 percent. Viewed from another perspective, before the crash, 1.5 million Americans were unemployed. By 1933, in the darkest days of the Depression, more than 13 million were unemployed. Also, over these 4 years, more than 5,000 banks failed and millions of Americans lost their savings due to the collapse of the banks. These economic developments affected American higher education in several ways.

First, because state tax receipts plummeted and social support programs became an urgent priority, public funding for public higher education was cut severely. A study examining the effects of the Great Depression found, in a survey of 198 public higher education institutions, that total institutional expenditures made during 1934 were less than those made in 1929 (Willey 1937). And funding for public higher education dropped from 22 percent of state budgets in 1930 to 14 percent in 1936 (Levine 1988). Some institutions experienced budget cuts that are almost unimaginable. For example, from 1931 to 1939, state appropriations to the University of California were reduced by 26 percent. And this occurred as enrollment increased 25 percent (Douglass 2000).

Second, one consequence of the financial pain inflicted on Americans was that the states began to take a second look at their educational institutions to see which might be eliminated in order to save money. Robert M. Hutchins, the President of the University of Chicago, addressed some of these proposals in December 1932 at his institution's convocation (Hutchins 1933). Hutchins acknowledged the growing call to close public high schools and public junior colleges in order to reduce the burden on state and local taxpayers. However, he enthusiastically rejected this proposal, arguing it would set back an entire generation and put many young people on the street without supervision. As a compromise, Hutchins suggested that the public high schools take over junior college instruction. Such a change would be justified, he thought, on both instructional and financial grounds. In his view, too many junior colleges were operating in isolation and many had failed to integrate their curricula with those offered at the universities. Additionally, folding junior college programs into public high schools would reduce administrative overhead. Hutchins' proposal was not systematically adopted in any jurisdiction. But it was certainly noticed and became a concern for many leaders in the junior college movement.

Third, during the hardest years of the Depression (1929–34), many students dropped out of college and returned home because their families were unable to pay their tuition bills. At the University of Chicago in the fall of 1931, 60 percent of the students who withdrew left for financial reasons (Levine 1988). Stanford University experienced its highest attrition rates since World War I. Some students leaving the university completely dropped out of higher education. But others enrolled at less expensive public junior colleges while living with their families at home. It is not surprising, therefore, that although overall student enrollment in American colleges and universities declined from 1931 to 1934, student enrollments at less expensive public junior colleges increased by 70 percent, from 30,000 to 51,000 (Allen and Allen 1937; Snyder 1993). During this period, the significant advantages of low cost and proximity made many high school graduates take a second look at the junior college. As one college administrator noted, "The junior college achieved its maximum usefulness during . . . the depression. It was in a better position . . . to fill the time of unemployed young people, to the benefit of themselves and of the state, than was any other unit of society" (Bracewell 1935, p. 517).

Fourth, the economic crisis placed a new priority on educational programs that provided students with skills needed for employment. Junior colleges were gradually moving to adopt more vocational curricula. But the Great Depression accelerated this trend. Hutchins addressed this subject as well at the December 1932 convocation. He argued for the creation of "a set of alternative courses of study, definitely terminal and not preparatory in character" that would provide students with instruction in technical fields and prepare them for employment, not university study (Hutchins 1933, p. 98). This technical education should be delivered through junior college programs at public high schools. What he was equally concerned with, however, was ensuring that the university did not enroll students seeking a technical education. As he explained, "they should not enter the university unless they have scholarly or professional interests" (Hutchins 1933, p. 98).

Fifth, the social and economic hardships created by the Great Depression led to the development of several federal programs to provide adults with educational opportunities in order to accelerate their return to the workforce. Most of these were administered under the authority of the Federal Emergency Relief Act (FERA), signed into law by President Franklin D. Roosevelt in May of 1933 (Greenleaf 1935; Reavis 1935; Schlesinger 1987). The Emergency Education Program, administered under FERA, distributed federal funding to junior colleges and other higher education institutions to accomplish three goals: (a) to provide financial aid to college students, (b) to deliver adult education programs, and (c) to deliver worker education programs. Junior colleges played a major role in helping the federal government accomplish its goals under the Emergency Education Program. As an example, during the fall 1934 academic term, 337 of the nation's 426 junior colleges were participating in the federal financial aid program and distributed federal funds to needy students each month in payment for their work at college.

In summary, the Great Depression had several important consequences for junior colleges. Their relatively low tuition led to an increase in enrollments. This increase in enrollment, the growing respect for vocational education programs, and prominent role in implementing federal relief programs reflected the rising profile of junior colleges in American higher education. Of course, traditionalists like Hutchins advocated for their return to public high school campuses. But this approach, although also endorsed by Koos, lost steam in the 1930s. What the Great Depression revealed was that the nation had a genuine need for low-cost postsecondary education and many adult learners were grateful for the opportunity to take college classes at the junior college. However, perhaps the most intriguing innovation in junior college education during this era was the creation of emergency junior colleges.

Emergency junior colleges

These institutions were created and funded through state and then federal emergency relief administrations (Bracewell 1935; Maddox 1934; Simpson 2007). And although they are seldom mentioned in the community college literature, they were not a minor or incidental innovation. During the early 1930s, federally funded emergency junior colleges were opened in New Jersey, Connecticut, Kansas, Texas, Ohio, and Michigan (Simpson 2007). The New Jersey experience was especially noteworthy.

In that state, in 1929, the legislature considered a bill to create public junior colleges but declined to move forward. Accordingly, New Jersey entered the Great Depression without any public 2-year institutions. As the severity of the crisis became evident, however, opposition to the institutions softened. Beginning in 1933, state relief officials established six emergency junior colleges. These colleges were opened with the support of the state's public and private universities (Morrison 1935; Simpson 2007). School districts leased facilities to the emergency junior colleges at no cost. Local and state education officials administered the colleges. Once operating, the salaries and other costs were funded with FERA dollars. And classes were offered to students without charge. Three programs of study were offered at the New Jersey colleges: arts and sciences, business administration, and engineering. Students completing coursework in business administration and engineering acquired vocational skills for the job market. Students completing coursework in the arts and sciences were prepared for transfer. Emergency junior college students succeeded in gaining admission at several colleges and universities including Georgetown, Bucknell, Rutgers, Dartmouth, Tulane, Colgate, and Brown.

Although ostensibly an educational institution, the colleges had two other purposes. The first was to hire unemployed teachers in order to keep people with teaching expertise ready for regular work once the economy recovered. The second was to provide unemployed young adults with the education needed to secure employment or admission at a university (Kennedy 2009; Morrison 1935; Outland 1937). The New Jersey emergency junior colleges existed for only 7 years. By the end of the decade, they had been merged into existing private institutions or closed (Morrison 1935; Simpson 2007).

The development of FERA-funded emergency junior colleges was not a national initiative. But in states like New Jersey, it was an important relief effort that affected the lives of thousands of instructors and students. The creation and operation of emergency junior colleges also affirmed that in desperate circumstances the federal government could and would subsidize open access, postsecondary institutions to address national, social, and economic needs.

Arguments for greater federal involvement in higher education

The Great Depression also changed the way Americans viewed the relationship between higher education and the federal government. Before the Depression, the states had jealously guarded their power and authority (granted by the Tenth Amendment to the United States Constitution) to establish and fund public higher education institutions. With the arrival of the Great Depression, however, it became clear that states were unable to adequately meet the society's higher education needs in times of severe crisis.

Noting this lack of capacity, in 1934 George Zook offered a blunt and critical assessment of the country's educational systems (Zook 1934). At the time, Zook was beginning his first term as the Director of the American Council on Education (ACE), a national advocacy group representing schools, colleges, and universities. Zook made two critical observations in this landmark work.

First, he observed that over the past three decades, the opportunities for students in elementary, secondary, and higher education had expanded substantially. However, this expansion had not been uniform and accordingly the nation suffered from an increase in inequality of education. The tolerance of poverty and racial discrimination, especially in the South, had left many students with only the most rudimentary educational experiences. This, in turn, meant that individual growth for many children and young adults was seriously limited. Second, inequality in educational opportunities was also a consequence of poor funding mechanisms. As was the tradition in the United States, most funding for public schools (approximately 80 percent) came from local and county governments. And the local and county tax revenues used to support education were almost always raised by a levy on real estate. Wealthy communities that had a high-value real estate tax base were able to collect much more revenue for education than those that had a low-value tax base. This disparity led to a significant difference in the quality of education delivered from one school district to the next. Furthermore, although real estate was a major source of wealth in the nineteenth century, the continuing industrialization in the early twentieth century meant that substantial wealth was being invested in corporate stocks and bonds and was not taxed by most local and county governments.

Because the funding of public education had not kept up with the growth in the economy and the United States did not have a national education policy, Zook concluded that the future of the nation was at risk. He argued that the remedy to this problem was more federal government involvement in education. Zook's call for more federal involvement occurred, of course, in the depths of the Great Depression when cities and states were pleading for financial assistance from the federal government. And yet, because the federal government had been only minimally involved in education, there were few administrative processes available to help the states. This created an appearance that state and federal governments were ineffective in maintaining a viable education system. This was a serious concern for Zook, in part because other advanced nations, facing similar problems precipitated by the Great Depression, were solving their problems by electing Fascist governments. And at least some of these governments appeared to be more effective in addressing national needs.

Of course, Zook recognized that the Tenth Amendment had long been interpreted as assigning the states primary responsibility for education. And he noted that the federal government's involvement in supporting education, although limited, was not well organized. But Washington had recently implemented several education relief initiatives that did accomplish important goals and this, he believed, demonstrated that the federal government could play a more active and constructive role in education. For the next decade, Zook would be an advocate for a more active federal role in education. He was a champion of the 1944 G. I. Bill, which was a major federal investment in education and 2 years later, he would chair President Truman's Commission on Higher Education, to which we turn in the next chapter. By the end of the 1930s, the nation was well on the road to accepting a new role for the federal government in American education. This new role was accepted not because the federal government had demonstrated a unique capacity to support education. It was accepted because, in a time of crisis, the states had failed to meet the needs of the society. They had failed to update their tax laws and turned a blind eye to the inequality in education that haunted much of the nation.

The junior college as the college for adults

The Great Depression and the changing role of the federal government were not the only developments that contributed to an increase in junior college enrollments during the 1930s. An equally important but more subtle development concerned the changing demographics of junior college students. The junior college student population of the 1920s and 1930s varied greatly from what we see today on community college campuses. Today, the average age of community college students is 28 years and 60 percent are enrolled on a part-time basis (AACC 2014 Fact Sheet). During the 1920s and 1930s, however, the vast majority of junior college students were recent graduates from high school (21 years and younger) and they attended class full time during the day (Eells 1931; Koos 1925; Zook 1926). In 1941, this aging of the junior college student population was addressed by Cyril Houle, a young professor who would go on to have a distinguished career in adult education (Houle 1941).

Houle observed that traditionally, junior colleges only operated day programs. But, now they were opening up new evening programs. Indeed, he found that 30 percent of all junior colleges were making arrangements to establish evening programs. The purpose of these new programs was to serve a new and rapidly expanding student population—adults (Houle 1941). For Houle, this marked an important milestone for junior colleges. He wrote that, "In developing these new activities, the junior college enters the broad field of adult education" (Houle 1941, p. 595). And adult education was very different from what junior colleges had been doing for the previous 40 years.

Houle noted that the junior college had a significant advantage when it came to serving this new population of learners. The junior college was a recent addition to American education, was less institutionalized, and therefore was more adaptable to change. Also, unlike other educational institutions, such as the high school and the university, the junior college had a more ambiguous identity and there was little preventing it from delivering a broad range of courses and programs, precisely the kind of program diversity that appealed to many adult learners.

Of course, adult education programs had been offered by a variety of organizations besides educational institutions (e.g., libraries, religious organizations, service clubs, and museums). But public junior colleges also had significant advantages when compared to these other adult education providers. Public junior colleges had an institutionalized revenue stream that afforded greater stability and security and education was the top priority for junior colleges, which suggested the institution might make a more permanent commitment to teaching adults.

Houle reminded his readers, that adult education was significantly different from the kind of teaching and learning that traditionally occurred in schools, colleges, and universities. Accordingly, if junior colleges continued to expand their enrollment of adult learners, their administrators, faculty, and staff would need to be mindful of two points. First, adult learning was not limited to the mastery of content delivered in a particular course or program. Adult learning synthesized new knowledge acquired in a course with valuable insights learned at work or in the community. The challenge to junior colleges, therefore, was to recognize that effective adult education required a respect for what adults learned outside the classroom. Ignoring the importance of learners' prior experience could easily bore and discourage busy adults who needed to see the real life relevancy of their classes.

Second, Houle argued that junior college leaders would need to carefully determine what programs they could best deliver and then leave the rest to others. Here Houle was simply acknowledging that no organization with limited resources could effectively provide a wide range of complex programs without sacrificing quality. Junior colleges, therefore, would need to make some difficult decisions in determining which programs should be offered to their new adult students and perhaps more importantly, which should not.

Despite these concerns, Houle affirmed the great potential of junior colleges to serve adult learners, especially those seeking vocational education programs. And, with the United States' entry into World War II in December 1941, the delivery of new adult vocational education programs—offering training for the defense industry—became a high priority for the nation and federal government.

Conclusion

During the 1930s, junior colleges gained new stature in the American higher education hierarchy. Although student enrollments decreased across higher education after the onset of the Great Depression, they increased at junior colleges because of their relatively low tuition, geographic proximity, and the growth of vocationally focused curricula. These new vocational programs were dismissed by some but respected by others eager to see a broadening of the curriculum. As junior colleges grew in stature and enrollment, private liberal arts colleges stumbled. They struggled financially and their leaders openly wondered whether they were the targets of an attack by public-sector institutions. Simultaneously, the adult education movement, which had exploded during the 1920s, began to stall in the 1930s because of its lack of organization, focus, and stable funding. Both of these developments gave junior colleges more space and time to become secure and settled.

Also, during the Great Depression, the federal role in directing and subsidizing postsecondary education expanded greatly. As Zook observed, state control of education had been a fundamental aspect of the American federal system. But when the financial crisis was at its worst, the states had failed to meet the educational needs of their citizens, balked at making the necessary reforms to fund education, and instead opted for a policy of austerity. There was an urgent need, Zook argued, for a greater federal role in education and under President Roosevelt, the federal government stepped into the breach. Junior colleges readily accepted responsibility for offering new adult education and worker education programs funded with FERA dollars. Leaders at the vast majority of these colleges agreed to distribute federal financial aid to needy students. Junior colleges also provided the organizational model and curricula for federal emergency institutions created to enroll (and also hire) the unemployed. Liberal arts colleges and universities certainly contributed to the nation's recovery from the Great Depression. But junior colleges, searching for a more secure and stable identity, took advantage of the crisis and aligned themselves with the needs and interests of the federal government.

By the end of the 1930s, the role of junior colleges in the American education hierarchy was more secure than it had been in the preceding 40 years. And they had made this progress while weathering the greatest social and economic domestic crisis of the twentieth century. The values and priorities that led them to this new success and stature need to be carefully noted, however. To be sure, junior colleges expanded their vocational offerings and took on responsibility for administering federal relief programs because of their desire to help students survive the Great Depression. But, noting the missteps of liberal arts colleges and the adult education movement, junior colleges also took on new responsibilities that served their institutional interests. The priority again was institutional survival, but with this becoming more certain, junior college leaders now turned to finding their place in the American higher education hierarchy. And, again, the critical values were flexibility, efficiency, accommodation, and service to other institutions. What junior colleges were also guided by, however, was a sense that they should serve the educational needs of the nation, as articulated by the federal government. After three decades of haphazard development under the auspices of many different public and private authorities, junior colleges, and specifically public junior colleges, had found their place in the American education hierarchy. And the Great Depression and federal government's effort to mitigate the crisis had been the catalysts.

6

The late twentieth century normative vision

Introduction

In this chapter I focus on a series of developments that shaped the evolution of junior colleges and then community colleges from 1940 to 1970. I begin by reviewing the influence of World War II on the junior colleges. An important development at the end of the war was the enactment of the GI Bill, which supported 2.2 million veterans who went to college after returning home. Then I discuss the Truman Commission Report of 1947, which laid out the federal government's vision for a new institution, the American community college. In 1960, the state of California adopted a Master Plan that assigned specific roles to the California Community College System, the California State University System, and the University of California System. The Master Plan accepted the vision for community colleges that had been articulated in the Truman Commission Report. But it added to this by explaining in detail how community colleges should operate in a hierarchical higher education system committed to both access and excellence. I next discuss two important pieces of federal legislation, the Higher Education Facilities Act of 1963 and the Higher Education Act of 1965. Both of these laws contributed to an increase in student enrollments across the country and this strengthened community colleges by granting them a permanent place in the American higher education hierarchy. For community colleges, the 30-year period from 1940 to 1970 was marked, like previous eras, by enrollment growth and an expanded role in the American higher education hierarchy. What most distinguished their growth and expanded role, however, was the active support of the federal government.

World War II

When Japanese warplanes bombed Pearl Harbor on December 7, 1941, Americans were shocked at the attack. But they were not surprised the nation was headed for combat against aggressive totalitarian regimes in Europe and Asia. Japan invaded China in the summer of 1937 and then it invaded the Soviet Union in July 1938. Nazi Germany's war machine invaded Poland in September 1939. In May 1940, German forces invaded France, Belgium, the Netherlands, and Luxembourg. In each of these cases, the military onslaught and occupation were accompanied by atrocities committed against civilians. In May 1941, a German U-boat torpedoed and sank the *Robin Moor*, an American freighter crossing the Atlantic. With the attack on Pearl Harbor, the World War had finally reached the United States and its territories.

The nation's higher education institutions responded to the increasing hostilities overseas by stepping up their preparation of young people for work in a wartime economy. After Pearl Harbor, however, they carried out this work while adjusting to a major decline in student enrollment. Both the Army and the Navy enlisted large numbers of young men and this significantly reduced enrollment at all colleges and universities. In 1940, total enrollment at American colleges and universities was 1.5 million. This fell steadily to 1.2 million in 1944, a decline of 20 percent before recovering in 1946 (Snyder 1993).

In 1940, one way the federal government prepared for military conflict was by establishing the Engineering, Science, and Management War Training Program (ESMWT) (Cardozier 1993). The ESMWT provided funding to more than 225 colleges and universities to train students for scientific and technical positions essential to a highly productive war economy. These courses were developed by college and university faculty in collaboration with industry leaders and federal officials. The ESMWT and similar federal training initiatives had significant consequences for many institutions. Colleges traditionally committed to the education of women (e.g., Wellesley, Skidmore, and Bryn Mawr) enrolled some of their first male students as a consequence of these programs. Also, Historically Black Colleges and Universities (HBCUs) offered ESMWT courses that significantly increased African American enrollments (Branson 1942). ESWMT courses were offered at universities, liberal arts colleges, and junior colleges (Cardozier 1993).

Higher education institutions contributed to the war effort in other ways too. The engineering and science faculty at universities conducted research that led to the development of radar, bomb sights, and the atom bomb (Abrams 1989). Working under secret contracts with the federal government, faculty at more than 25 universities helped develop biological and chemical weapons (Abrams 1989). Liberal arts colleges offered courses focusing on "the

American idea" and "the heritage of the United States" (Kallen 1942, p. 339). Teachers colleges developed supplemental short-term courses to refresh and strengthen teachers' knowledge of subjects essential for a wartime workforce producing armaments.

Junior colleges also made adjustments in order to build morale, support the United States military, and train defense contractor employees. For example, in Connecticut, soon after the Japanese bombing of Pearl Harbor, New Haven YMCA Junior College began offering in-service training courses for the employees of area defense contractors (Bethel and Wilson 1942). In Chicago, in February 1942, Woodrow Wilson Junior College invited guest speakers to campus who lectured on civil defense administration (Berolzheimer 1942). San Francisco Junior College, potentially on the front lines in the event of an invasion, offered 32 new courses such as "Winning the War, Civilian Defense, Weather Elements, Map Interpretation, Practical Air Navigation" (Wartime Activities 1943). Sixteen junior colleges hosted Reserve Officer Training Corps programs and another 126 served as Pilot Training Centers under the direction of the Civil Aeronautics Administration (Wartime Activities 1942a). Some junior college campuses were seized by the military through condemnation proceedings. For example, National Park College, a private junior college located in Forest Glen, Maryland, was taken over by the Army in August 1942 for use as medical facilities because of its proximity to Walter Reed Hospital (Wartime Activities 1942b).

The Japanese attack on an important US territory raised anxiety across the United States and the federal government was ceded unusually broad powers to mount a defense of the nation. This power had a significant impact on colleges and universities. The military drafted college students for the military, used campus facilities for training, contracted with universities for research, and in some cases, completely took over institutions when they were needed for military activities. Seventy years after the war, it is easy to forget the impact the federal government had on colleges and universities during the crisis. But this impact was substantial and could have been much greater. In the fall of 1942, *Time* magazine reported that some in Washington believed the Army and Navy might "take over the colleges lock, stock & barrel" to prepare young men for the war effort (Who Will Run the Colleges? 1942, p. 83). And, the *Time* correspondent added, "college presidents heard disquieting reports that the Army & Navy planned to use fewer than 500 of the 1,700 colleges; the rest might have to give up for the duration" (Who Will Run the Colleges? 1942, p. 83). We may never know how close the nation came to a massive takeover of civilian colleges and universities. But there was little that would have stopped the federal government, had officials decided such extraordinary measures were necessary.

The Servicemen's Readjustment Act of 1944 (the GI Bill)

When World War II ended in August 1945, the nation entered a period of great social readjustment. During the war, 43 million Americans had registered for military duty and more than 16 million had actually served (Kennedy 1999; Patterson 1997). Political leaders understood that reintegrating these soldiers and sailors into civilian life would be a huge undertaking (Loss 2012). It is also important to note that the 16 million who served constituted more than 10 percent of the nation's total population in 1940, approximately 132 million (Bureau of the Census 1942).

Policymakers like George Zook were especially concerned with the need to provide veterans with educational benefits. Zook and his colleagues argued that educational benefits for veterans were important for two reasons. First, the country needed to recover from the educational deficit it suffered when many young adults left college to go to war. Second, the nation had a moral duty to help veterans pursue an education. Zook's arguments were persuasive. Congressional leaders moved legislation through both houses in the winter of 1944 and on June 22, 1944, President Roosevelt signed the GI Bill. The law supported veterans with financial assistance if they were unable to find work. It also provided them with low-interest loans to purchase a home, business, or farm. And the GI Bill provided veterans with cash to pay for tuition and living expenses if they enrolled in college. Eight million veterans would eventually take advantage of the GI Bill and of these, 2.2 million used the educational benefits. Of course, this led to a substantial increase in student enrollments. In 1940, 1.5 million students were enrolled in higher education. By 1950 just under 2.3 million were enrolled, almost a 55 percent increase (Snyder 1993). The enrollment increase at junior colleges, in particular, was also substantial. In 1940, junior colleges enrolled 150,000 students. Ten years later, 218,000 students were taking classes at junior colleges, a 45 percent increase (Snyder 1993).

In January 1946, at a meeting of the American Association of Junior Colleges (AAJC), junior college leaders reflected on how their institutions had fared during the war and how the GI Bill would affect them in the future (Fine 1946). They noted that because of declining enrollments during the war, more than 100 junior colleges had been forced to close. But with the new GI Bill in effect, AAJC leaders predicted that the 600 surviving institutions would be unable to handle the anticipated increase in student enrollments over the next 10 years. Accordingly, AAJC leaders called for the establishment of an additional 300 to 500 junior colleges. At the time, junior college leaders were primarily concerned with the anticipated enrollment increases due to the

GI Bill. But this incentive to go to college was soon complemented by a new report from the federal government that recommended a dramatic expansion of higher education opportunities for all Americans.

The Truman Commission Report

The ending of World War II, the reconstruction of Europe and Japan, and the first signs of a Cold War with the Soviet Union led American leaders to call for a larger federal role in education. In July 1946, President Truman responded by establishing a commission to determine the nation's higher education needs. Truman appointed 28 civic and educational leaders and asked them to consider a number of issues. He specifically asked them to investigate:

> ways and means of expanding educational opportunities for all able young people; the adequacy of curricula, particularly in the fields of international affairs and social understanding; the desirability of establishing a series of intermediate technical institutes; the financial structure of higher education with particular reference to the requirements for the rapid expansion of physical facilities. (President's Commission on Higher Education 1947, Volume I, p. iv)

The President's charge reflected the widely held belief that American higher education needed to reform itself in order to prepare the next generation for the atomic age.

In December 1947, the Commission delivered its six-volume report. Contrary to the conventional wisdom of the late 1940s, the Truman Commission Report characterized higher education as an experience that should be within the grasp of every able American. To carry out this overarching objective, the report offered ten recommendations. The most important of these were the following: (a) the elimination of racial segregation in student admissions and enrollment, (b) the creation of a federally funded undergraduate student scholarship program (based primarily on need), (c) federally funded fellowships for graduate study, (d) the elimination of tuition for students enrolled in the first 2 years of college, and (e) the establishment of "free, public, community colleges" which would offer transfer programs, vocational education programs, and, for students with remedial needs, adult education programs (President's Commission on Higher Education 1947, Volume I, p. 69).

The members of the Truman Commission were well aware that historically higher education had been a responsibility of the states. But given the experience of the 1930s, the new needs of the nation, and the challenges they saw emerging, the Commission recommended a much larger role for the federal government. And along with this, the Truman Commission asked the states to pick up the pace in developing their higher education systems. In particular, the Commission recommended that states conduct research on the educational needs of their adults, prepare state-wide plans on improving public higher education, and establish state coordinating boards for public colleges and universities. Supporters viewed the report's recommendations as bold and visionary.

However, Robert M. Hutchins, the President at the University of Chicago, described the Commission's report as, "big and booming. It is confused, confusing, and contradictory" (Hutchins 1948, p. 107). In regard to the community college recommendation, Hutchins added that although the institution could provide greater access to higher education, beyond this, serious questions remained. Hutchins concluded, "the Commission has no clear idea of the purpose, organization, or activities of the community college" (Hutchins 1948, p. 107).

This new federal role in higher education, as a source for funding, as the advocate for nondiscriminatory admission practices, and as a powerful stimulant for new state higher education reforms deeply troubled some on the Commission. Two members, Dr Martin R. P. McGuire and Mgr Frederick G. Hochwalt, dissented from much of the report. In their dissent, they warned readers that some of the Commission's recommendations "would go a long way toward establishing an administrative structure for higher education whereby Government in the United States might easily use the nation's public colleges and universities to promote its political purposes" (President's Commission on Higher Education 1947, Volume V, p. 66). Commissioners McGuire and Hochwalt did not explain what they meant by "political purposes." But they recognized that making education more of a federal priority brought certain tradeoffs with it. Any financial advantages to be gained in the near future might be offset down the road when the federal government decided to promote other priorities.

The Truman Commission was clearly ahead of its time and some of its recommendations would not be fully implemented for decades (e.g., ending racially segregated institutions in the South). But it quickly gave public 2-year institutions a new federally approved identity and institutional legitimacy. The new identity enabled junior colleges to step beyond their traditional role of offering transfer programs. It legitimized the delivery of new vocational and adult education programs. Of course, the vocationalization of the curriculum had been underway for at least two decades. But the Truman Commission's recommendation gave new energy to this unfolding change in the curriculum.

As many readers know, the formal change in the name of institutions from "junior college" to "community college" would also take time. Some 2-year institutions would continue to be identified as junior colleges (or technical colleges) for the next 50 years. But the community college identity—as an open access, comprehensive, publicly funded institution—was clearly articulated and validated in the Truman Commission Report. This new identity also provided community colleges with a legitimacy, not only in academia but in the community as well.

Finally, the Truman Commission's call for creating a new system of community colleges was also driven by a vision of education and democracy that must be acknowledged. The Nazi regime defeated in World War II came to power through democratic means and the authors of The Truman Commission Report understood that in a democratic nation, education must be much more than a mechanism to prepare people for leisure, work, and the voting booth. It must prepare everyone for life in a democracy. The authors of the report wrote

> Democracy is much more than a set of political processes. It formulates and implements a philosophy of human relations. It is a way of life—a way of thinking, feeling, and acting, in regard to the associations of men and of groups, one with another. . . . To educate our citizens only in the structure and processes of the American government, therefore, is to fall far short of what is needed for the fuller realization of the democratic ideal. It is the responsibility of higher education to devise programs and methods which will make clear the ethical values and the concept of human relations upon which our political system rests. (President's Commission on Higher Education 1947, Volume I, pp. 11–12)

The Truman Commission Report was not the only example of the federal government's new involvement in higher education after World War II (Loss 2012). Also in 1947, the President's Commission on Civil Rights issued a report which recommended, among other things, the end to racial segregation across higher education. By 1950, federal funding of research projects at universities had reached an all-time high, even exceeding what had been spent on university research during World War II. Considered collectively, the GI Bill, the Truman Commission Report, the recommendations of the President's Commission on Civil Rights, the infusion of federal research dollars, and significant enrollment growth all signaled a new era in higher education. It is not surprising that many in academia looked back on the late 1940s and the 1950s as a "golden age" (Loss 2012, p. 123). To be sure, the golden age transcended all of American higher education. The new status of public 2-year institutions was just one example of the nation's new commitment to invest in higher education. But community colleges had the most to gain, and they did. The new role for community colleges, as an essential component of American higher education, was demonstrated most clearly in California.

The California Master Plan

During the late 1950s, student enrollment growth and encouragement from the federal government led many states to develop new higher education coordinating systems. The primary purpose of these administrative systems was to help the state manage costs while expanding capacity (Douglass 2000). The new coordinating systems often had significant consequences for community colleges because they confirmed their location in the state's higher education hierarchy. One of the states that created a new coordinating system was California.

California's population growth and its geographic size posed a serious challenge to administrators charged with coordinating a range of different institutions. Three aspects of this challenge are worth noting. First, in terms of population, in 1960 California was exceptional. It was the nation's second largest state with 15.7 million residents (United States Census Bureau 1961). (New York was the nation's largest with 16.8 million residents.) Also, California's population increase from 1950 (10.6 million) to 1960 (15.7 million) was approximately 48 percent. This rate of increase surpassed that of every other state in the nation with the exception of Florida. Second, in 1950, California had the largest number of public colleges and universities in the nation, with 55 junior and community colleges, 12 state colleges, and 2 campuses in the University of California system (Callan 2009). This total of 69 public institutions would increase to 86 by 1960. Also, unlike geographically smaller states that could handle enrollment increases by adding capacity at existing institutions, California's large area required the construction of new institutions to serve students in the regions where they lived. Third, when compared to other states, especially those located in the traditional Northeast, California was a large state relying heavily on a large public higher education system to serve a rapidly growing population. It is not surprising, therefore, that the state would struggle to develop a long-range plan that would achieve both access and academic excellence (Douglass 2000).

In 1959 and 1960, representatives from higher education, public education, and state government worked in teams to develop a plan for coordinating the state's public higher education institutions. At the beginning of the negotiations, a clear division separated (a) the University of California from (b) the California state colleges (now campuses in the California State University System) and the public junior colleges. This division was grounded in the institutions' different governing authorities and institutional missions. First, state oversight for both the state colleges and public junior colleges was carried out by the state department of education, the same agency responsible for state administration of public schools. The University of California, on the other hand, was governed by an independent board of regents. Second, the University of California was identified as the state's primary research institution and it alone had authority to award doctoral degrees. Given these circumstances, it was not surprising negotiations bogged down when advocates for the state colleges asked for authority to conduct research and award some doctoral degrees.

Although the state's need for a new higher education system was critical, the conflict between the state colleges and the University of California threatened to scuttle the negotiations on several occasions. Eventually, a compromise was adopted that led to the state legislature's passing the Donahoe Act, a bill articulating the major provisions of a new Master Plan for California higher education. Governor Pat Brown signed the bill in April 1960. The compromise settled the major disputes and laid down an organizational framework for California higher education that, in its major features, survives to this day (Douglass 2000).

Under the terms of the Donahoe Act, the mission of the University of California as the state's primary research institution was secured. The University of California would also retain authority for offering bachelor's, master's, doctoral, and professional degree programs. Its campuses would become more selective at the undergraduate level, admitting the top 12.5 percent of in-state high school graduates, when they previously had been admitting the top 15 percent. And, to accommodate enrollment growth, the new law authorized the development of three new University of California campuses at San Diego, Santa Cruz, and Irvine.

The mission of the California State University campuses was also clarified. The CSU institutions would continue to offer bachelor's and master's degrees and now they would be permitted to carry out some research. And, although the CSU institutions had previously admitted the top 40 percent of in-state high school graduates, their undergraduate programs would now become more selective and admit only the top 33.3 percent. The Donahoe Act also established a new governing board for the state colleges and approved four new CSU campuses to be located in San Bernadino, Stanislaus, Hayward, and Northridge.

The state's community colleges would retain their authority to offer associate's degrees and deliver adult and vocational programs. Additionally, because community colleges would assume a larger share of future enrollments, legislators agreed that over the next 15 years, the state's portion of their annual operating budget would be increased from 30 to 45 percent. Finally, because of this anticipated enrollment growth, 22 new community college campuses were proposed and plans for these began to move forward through the state planning process.

The Donahoe Act and the resulting 1960 Master Plan were major developments in the evolution of the nation's largest public higher education system. This large but well-coordinated system became a justifiable source of pride for California educators and policymakers. Until recently, California has delivered on promises to offer accessible and high quality higher education to its residents. However, the 1960 Master Plan also entailed decisions that reinforced a service identity for the community colleges.

For example, during the negotiation of the 1960 Master Plan, the biggest dispute concerned a hierarchical challenge that the state's 4-year colleges posed to the University of California. The state colleges wanted more independence. They also wanted more prestige. In the end, both the UC and the new CSU institutions moved ahead in creating more selective and prestigious institutions. An essential condition of these advancements, however, was that the state's community colleges would enroll a larger share of the undergraduate population. There was no serious suggestion that students with low and moderate academic records would be better educated at the community colleges. The community colleges did not have more resources or better faculty. They were simply more accessible and less expensive to operate. What community colleges would be faced with, therefore, was the increasingly difficult task of managing commitments to open access and an expanding vocational curriculum, while also taking on greater responsibility for working with students unable to proceed on to university coursework. This filtering responsibility, which was a significant but informal feature of the nation's early junior colleges, became a more dominant and formal feature of community colleges in California and throughout the nation. Community colleges accepted this responsibility because it secured their place in American higher education. But the place it secured was subordinate to the universities.

Federal legislation promoting the growth and expansion of higher education

During the 1950s and 1960s, the federal government began a series of major program initiatives to educate more American adults. These initiatives emerged from new social and political commitments to end poverty, to end racial discrimination, and to produce a population with the knowledge and skills needed to secure the United States' superpower status assumed at the close of World War II. In the beginning, the focus of these initiatives was on supporting the defense industries and stimulating economic growth (Hansen 1983). For example, the National Defense Education Act of 1958 (NDEA) provided federal funding for programs implemented across the education spectrum, from elementary school through postgraduate studies

(Loss 2012). Under the NDEA, Congress appropriated funds to expand the use of television in the classroom, to develop foreign language and international study centers, and to support graduate fellowships for study in the sciences and mathematics. Also, between 1959 and 1969, approximately 1.5 million students went to college on NDEA loans. This attention to national defense and economic growth was soon matched by another priority, however, and this was the social justice agenda of the 1960s.

Following the assassination of President John F. Kennedy in November 1963, the promotion of civil rights and the expansion of educational opportunity became the two central higher education policy priorities for the new administration. In 1964, with strong backing from President Lyndon B. Johnson, the Congress passed the landmark 1964 Civil Rights Act. This law prohibited discrimination in housing, employment, and travel, based on race, sex, religion, and national origin. Also, the 1964 Civil Rights Act prohibited discrimination by institutions receiving federal funds and this included almost all colleges and universities. The implementation of the law was obstructed at some colleges and universities. Some aspects of desegregation took decades to accomplish. Still, over the next twenty years, the federal government worked to enforce provisions of the 1964 Civil Rights Act in many higher education settings.

In 1965, President Johnson signed the Higher Education Act of 1965 (the HEA) which further extended the role of the federal government in supporting and regulating American higher education (Archibald 2002; Loss 2012). Johnson, a former educator and inspired by the New Deal as a young man, was a strong supporter of the educational opportunity promised by the HEA. The 1965 law had several critical objectives. First, it authorized financial assistance to colleges and universities to help build and renovate campus facilities. Second, the HEA authorized funding to prepare teachers for work in poverty-stricken and underserved parts of the country. Third, and most importantly for us, however, the law authorized four student financial aid programs.

Two of these, a student work-study program and a direct student loan program for persons working in defense-related fields, were continuations of earlier federal programs. However, two new programs were created to provide opportunities for student populations previously underrepresented in higher education (Orfield 1990). The first was a new federal basic educational opportunity grant program, later known as the Pell Grant program. It provided financial assistance to low-income college students who had not yet received a bachelor's degree. The second was a new guaranteed student loan program for students from low-income families. Although these low-interest guaranteed loans were initially limited to low-income students, changes to the law in 1972, 1978, and 1992 opened up the program to almost all students without regard to family income (Cofer and Somers 2001; Naegele 1983).

In addition to the four student financial aid programs, the HEA authorized college preparatory programs to help low-income and minority students' transition to college. Perhaps the best-known college prep initiative was Upward Bound, which brought high school students to college campuses during the summer to familiarize them with the culture and academics of college life. This early exposure to college life enabled many low-income and minority students to see how they could fit into a culture that was an unknown to many of them. The HEA had a great impact on colleges, universities, and their students. As Christopher Loss explained, "The HEA transformed American higher education . . . [and] changed the way college administrators crafted student bodies and how all students financed their educations" (Loss 2012, p. 178). For community colleges, the increasing federal support for higher education had critical positive consequences. As I explain later, the increase in funding for low-income students greatly increased the amount of federal support going to community colleges. The point for now, however, is that these federal laws underscored the nation's commitment to educational opportunity and this dovetailed with recommendations made in the Truman Commission Report. By 1970, community colleges were an established component in state higher education systems. Their mission of providing access to students interested in transfer and vocational curricula was neatly aligned with federal higher education legislation and civil rights legislation that emphasized an expansion of educational opportunity.

Conclusion

Public junior colleges acquired a new identity and legitimacy after World War II as a result of the GI Bill and the Truman Commission Report. This new identity and legitimacy aligned closely with national educational priorities (e.g., expanding educational opportunity and developing a workforce for the Cold War). In California, the development of community colleges and the community college system occurred for the same and also different reasons. The promotion of a higher education system capable of enhancing educational opportunity was a high priority. But the Master Plan assigned community colleges the essential role of enrolling students not yet ready for university study. Many states adopted similar higher education systems with the same priorities and hierarchical division of responsibility. Community colleges followed through on the federal government's promise to expand educational opportunity. They also helped the states operate a higher education system that balanced access, efficiency, and academic excellence. But the long-term financial and social consequences of such a system were seldom calculated.

7

Turning to a new normative vision

Introduction

During the 1960s and 1970s, the mainstays of the community college curriculum were transfer programs and new vocational programs. Community colleges also took the lead in delivering courses in the evening, on the weekend, off campus, and under new extended schedules for part-time students. Fueled by these internal innovations, the new federal financial aid programs, and heavy state investment in educational facilities, community college enrollments exploded. More specifically, enrollments grew from 900,000 in 1964 to 2.0 million in 1969 and then up to 3.3 million in 1974 (Snyder and Dillow 2011). Across the country, public 2-year institutions were fulfilling the promise of higher educational opportunity. Enrollments at community colleges would continue to grow for the next 40 years. But the rate of growth would never exceed the boom years of the 1960s and 1970s. In 1984, community college enrollments totaled 4.3 million. In 1994, the numbers grew to 5.3 million and then extended to 6.2 million in 2004. In 2014, enrollments were projected to reach 8.0 million.

Heavy government investment during the late 1940s and 1950s led to the golden age of American higher education. But the enrollment growth of the 1960s and 1970s also made this period a magical time for community colleges. The community colleges were in sync with the nation's progressive movements seeking civil rights for African Americans, equal rights for women, and an end to poverty. It was during these years, however, that researchers started to look more critically at how community colleges were managing their enrollments.

This chapter begins by revisiting landmark student diversion studies completed by Clark in 1960 and then Brint and Karabel in 1989. After examining the student diversion studies, I focus on a critically important AACC policy document, *Building Communities: A Vision for a New Century* published in 1988.

The *Building Communities* Report acknowledged that the American economy was becoming more globalized and that as a result, many communities were facing economic decline and chronically high unemployment as employers moved their production facilities overseas. The consequence was that many parts of the nation were becoming increasingly polarized: economically, socially, and educationally. The authors of *Building Communities* argued that community colleges had a central role to play in helping the nation fight off this decline and polarization. They proposed, therefore, a new vision for community colleges—community development. Although this vision was well grounded empirically and articulated with passion, it failed to redirect community colleges in the last decade of the twentieth century or in the first decade of the twenty-first century. The economic and social problems identified in *Building Communities* continued and in some cases worsened and I explain the consequences for public higher education. During this era, many states, unable to meet their fiscal commitments, cut funding for public higher education and passed along the rising costs to students. This period of continuing decline and polarization took on crisis proportions during the Financial Crisis of 2007–08 and the Great Recession of 2007–09. It was during these crisis years that much of the nation lost its passion for expanding educational opportunity. Finally, I offer a critical review of *Reclaiming the American Dream: Community Colleges and the Nation's Future* (2012), the AACC report that proposed a new normative vision for community college education incorporating the national economic priorities of achieving greater economic growth and reducing income inequality.

As I mentioned above, my account of the last 45 years is not offered as a comprehensive account of the evolution of community colleges. This period was marked by countless successes that I do not address. These include the development of new vocational programs, the delivery of dual enrollment programs, the emergence and rapid growth of online education, the advent of civic engagement programs, the creation of new placement testing and developmental studies programs, and the arrival of better trained and more proficient instructional, student development, and administrative staff. These successes have been unambiguous. But along with these, has been the continuing and now decades-long struggle to move beyond a normative vision that focuses on the expansion of educational opportunity. This chapter reviews critical milestones during this period.

The student diversion studies

In 1960, a young sociologist at the University of California, Berkeley reported findings from a case study he completed at San Jose Junior College (SJJC), a community college in San Jose, California (Clark 1960a). Burton Clark found that when SJJC transfer students faltered in their transfer courses, faculty and staff used a variety of advising practices to support them. These practices, however, also alerted students to the possibility that they may fail in their studies. Clark observed that practices such as academic warnings and counseling gradually informed students that the transfer curriculum may not be for them. When students asked for recommendations on how to proceed, they were often referred to a vocational program. Usually transfer students would take the advice and transition to the vocational program, avoid academic failure, and move into a new career path.

Clark found that these advising practices effectively diverted students out of the transfer program and away from future university study. But these practices also helped students reset their goals. In other words, students struggling in academic courses would gradually accept that the transfer curriculum and the future challenges of university coursework may be too much for them to handle. Seeing vocational programs as a good alternative, students would leave the transfer program and set their sights on a new, albeit less prestigious, career. Clark noted that this process not only diverted students into less challenging vocational programs, it also helped manage a serious challenge to American society.

Clark explained that in the United States, the society had an important interest in encouraging young people to excel. This encouragement helped ensure that a sufficient number of engineers, scientists, and professionals would be available in the future. Of course, not every student interested in such a career could achieve this success—there were simply not enough of these jobs in the labor market. Also, many students had not been prepared for the rigorous course of study leading to these professions. Accordingly, the nation required a process whereby ambitious students could pursue educational opportunities, but then could be redirected if they did not succeed in their studies. And, most importantly, in order for a nation's higher education system to perform this work without provoking civil unrest, students would need to accept their fate without seriously questioning whether they had been treated fairly.

Clark found that SJJC was very effective in handling this dual responsibility of providing students with educational opportunities while also diverting low performers out of the transfer program. For Clark, however, this work included an element of deception. He called this diversionary process "cooling out," a term used in the gambling business to explain how casinos convinced inexperienced bettors that they alone were responsible for their losses. What Clark was saying, therefore, was that junior colleges were created, in part, to help manage the tension that inevitably arises when society's encouragement to excel results in a competition for a limited number of attractive career opportunities where there are winners and losers.

Clark's 1960 "cooling out" article reported on a pathbreaking study on the community college. Sociologists discussed the article at conferences and in many later journal articles. But Clark's study was not well received on community college campuses. No community college instructor wanted to think of his advising work as deceptive. No community college student wanted to believe that he was tracked into a vocational program as a result of a manipulative advising process that subtly reset his hopes and dreams. Nevertheless, Clark's "cooling out" article has never been refuted. Clark's study, although limited and concise, accurately described a process that happened routinely at community colleges in the 1950s and 1960s. And cooling out still happens at community colleges today. The faculty and staff doing this work today would hasten to add that their only motivation is to provide students with educational options. And this is certainly true. But the system in which they operate balances the promotion of educational opportunity with the needs of an educational meritocracy and it does so on the backs of community college students who have not yet realized the significant gap between their goals and their abilities.

The process Clark described worked well for many in higher education. University faculty were spared the labor of working with underprepared students. Community colleges moved students from one program to another and retained their enrollment funding. Employers were provided with employees trained and subsidized by the state. The American society could encourage students to excel while avoiding a crisis in unmet expectations. However, community college students diverted into vocational programs lived with the long-term consequences of a blue-collar career. Thirty years later, another study described this phenomenon, from another perspective, as a part of a larger historical development in American higher education.

In 1989, Steven Brint and Jerome Karabel, two sociologists at Yale University and the University of California, Berkeley, respectively, published *The Diverted Dream: Community Colleges and the Promise of Educational Opportunity in America, 1900–1985* (Brint and Karabel 1989). Brint and Karabel reviewed the evolution of junior colleges and their transformation into community colleges. They also explained how junior colleges gradually expanded their vocational education programs to secure their place in the higher education hierarchy. The authors acknowledged that when communities established a new junior college, a higher percentage of high school graduates from the area attended college. Students attended junior colleges because they were nearby, had lower admissions standards, and the tuition was less than that charged by traditional 4-year colleges and universities. Accordingly, it was true, as many junior college advocates had argued, that these new institutions democratized higher education by increasing overall college student enrollment.

However, Brint and Karabel also found that as junior colleges and then community colleges grew, they diverted academically prepared students away from traditional 4-year colleges and universities where they had a higher probability of completing the bachelor's degree. And, Brint and Karabel reported, students diverted to community colleges were often encouraged to enroll in vocational education programs. Students graduating from these programs usually ended up in low-wage, blue-collar careers as opposed to those who enrolled initially at a 4-year college or university, completed a bachelor's degree, and then went on to a white-collar professional career. Therefore, the sociologists argued, the diversion of underprepared and low-income students from a 4-year institution to a community college effectively replicated the status quo in the workforce. Although junior colleges and then community colleges were often praised as an American institution that improved social mobility, Brint and Karabel's research found that the story was actually more complicated. In some cases, community colleges limited social mobility.

Like Clark's study, Brint and Karabel's *The Diverted Dream* received a cool reception on community college campuses. Community college faculty, staff, and administrators understood that students enrolling at 4-year institutions were more likely to graduate with a bachelor's degree than those attending a community college. But, for them, the comparison rested on a false premise. They knew that most students attended community colleges because they had no other option. Asserting that students attending a community college were less likely to complete a bachelor's degree was a bit like arguing that Columbus would have discovered "The New World" more quickly if he had taken a speedboat. Maybe so. But that was never an option.

Community college practitioners also argued there was more than a whiff of hypocrisy in the air when professors at elite universities pointed to the lowly community college as responsible for crushing the dreams of underprepared students unable to gain admission at a university. What these practitioners knew was that many of their transfer students would have gained admission to a university, had the society invested more resources in the high schools these students attended.

In fairness to Clark and also Brint and Karabel, they never contended that the distribution of resources in American education was fair or equitable. In fact, they argued the reverse was true. They did not deny that elite universities were the beneficiaries of an unfair hierarchical system that reinforced the class structure in American society. But their arguments, although made with sensitivity and respect for community colleges, were often misread and this led to a circling of the wagons on community college campuses.

The larger point to be made here is that whether community colleges were diverting students from one program to another or from one institution to another, the diversion routed students away from white-collar careers and into blue-collar jobs. Clark and then Brint and Karabel highlighted an important but unfortunate truth about community college education that became more visible as these institutions became bureaucratized in large state systems. Community colleges played a critically important role in American higher education by rationalizing a class hierarchy that pervaded American society, including its colleges and universities. This rationalization enabled some to argue that low-income and underprepared students were not denied a shot at the American Dream. These students always had the opportunity of enrolling at a community college and then moving on to a university where they could climb the ladder to the middle class. What these students usually did not fully understand, however, was that the same institution affording them a convenient and low-cost education was also securing and validating a hierarchical system of higher education.

Today, every community college can identify students who have transferred to a university and then graduated with a bachelor's degree. Some go on and become successful in business or one of the professions. But these success stories do not compensate for what many Americans also now know to be a painful truth. Most students who come to the community college intending to transfer and then graduate with a bachelor's degree, do not. What Clark and Brint and Karabel told us and what many of us now know from our own experience is this: although community colleges provide students with important educational opportunities, these same institutions play a vital role in maintaining the status quo and securing a fundamentally unfair system of higher education. In this system, students from affluent communities generally receive a much better high school education and have many opportunities to prepare for college. But, students from poor communities usually receive a much more limited secondary education and are usually less prepared for college. Unfortunately, for many students, the long term negative consequences of this inequality become a reality at a community college.

Building communities:
A vision for a new century

Over the last 25 years, the evolution of community colleges has been influenced by two major national policy statements released by AACC. The first was published in 1988, the second in 2012. In 1986, AACC established a study group, the Commission on the Future of Community Colleges, and charged it with assessing the current status of community colleges and then making recommendations to guide their development in the future. The Commission was comprised of community college leaders, university researchers, state legislators, and policy analysts. In April 1988, the Commission issued its final report, *Building Communities: A Vision For A New Century* (*Building Communities*) (AACC 1988).

The authors of *Building Communities* explained how the rapid enrollment growth at community colleges, peaking during the 1960s and 1970s, had leveled off. Providing access, although still the top priority, was no longer the overriding or dominate priority it had been in the past. Now, new priorities were also emerging. At the forefront of these new priorities, the Commission argued, was the need for community colleges to focus on "building communities" which meant supporting communities in college service areas but also creating a cooperative and collaborative climate on campus. There were two reasons for this broad recommendation.

First, the Commission on the Future observed that the nation was challenged by a series of serious domestic problems. These included (a) a breakdown in the social life of neighborhoods, (b) an increase in class, racial, and ethnic polarization, (c) the inability of public schools to adequately serve an increasingly at-risk student population, (d) rising unemployment, (e) a decline in civic literacy, (f) the arrival of the Information Age which required substantial new skill training in the workplace, and (g) a failure of the states to fund community colleges at rates comparable to those provided for other public colleges and universities.

Second, community colleges faced their own significant institutional problems. These were (a) a growing division between administrators and faculty and the absence of inclusive decision-making arrangements, (b) a shortage of creative community college leadership development programs, (c) the employment of too many adjuncts which placed institutional culture and effectiveness at risk, (d) a fragmented curriculum which denied students a holistic general education experience, and (e) the loss of institutional vitality "precisely because there is no vision widely shared" (AACC 1988, p. 29).

Despite these serious concerns, the authors of *Building Communities* remained optimistic about the future and noted that the nation and its community colleges were "inextricably interlocked" (AACC 1988, p. 49). What was needed, the Commission argued, was a new vision focused on building, or in some cases rebuilding, communities. This would require a series of efforts both on and off campus. To rebuild the community on campus, colleges would need to achieve excellence in instruction, improve their use of technology, update their vocational programs, develop a common core curriculum for all students, develop new assessment programs, streamline the transfer process, strengthen professional development programs, and recommit themselves to lifelong learning. To help build the community off campus, the Commission called upon college leaders to establish better partnerships and alliances with schools, 4-year colleges and universities, and employers.

The *Building Communities* report is also noteworthy because the authors declined to endorse the growing sentiment that higher education should be viewed in economic terms. The authors wrote,

> At a time when society's values are shaped and revised by the fashion of the marketplace, the influence of the community college must grow outward from a core of integrity and confidence firmly rooted in humane goals that are currently lacking in too many of our societal institutions. (AACC 1988, p. 49)

The Commission on the Future recognized that the challenges outlined in their report were daunting. But, they argued, an economic logic—as applied to decision-making in higher education—was not the answer. The vision they advocated, to guide community colleges into the twenty-first century, was one grounded in the notion of building communities.

Building Communities was a milestone report that sought to build on the success of the traditional community college mission. Since World War II, community colleges had been aligned with a national educational policy committed to expanding educational opportunity. This was still the top priority after *Building Communities.* But, by the end of the twentieth century, life in America was changing and social scientists noted there was a broad-based sense of decline in American communities (Putnam 2000). The authors of *Building Communities* articulated this concern concisely, but as well as anyone else. They argued that the decline of American communities was a nation-wide problem. The remedy was for community colleges to help rebuild them.

Today, as we look back, it is evident *Building Communities* recommended a number of on-campus and off-campus strategies to address the problems it identified. But, it declined to go any farther than recommending that community colleges should do a better job of what they were already doing. *Building Communities* balked at recommending an institution-wide transformation of community colleges. The report did not clearly articulate the values underlying "building communities" and explain how these were relevant to students' individual lives. Yes, the authors wrote, twenty-first-century community colleges should value diversity, collaboration, service, participation, effective teaching, and lifelong learning. But *Building Communities* did not provide a convincing vision of how or why building communities would be integrated with enhancing educational opportunity. And the report had little to say about the American democracy or what democratic life in a community should be. Finally, it is also evident that *Building Communities* was never supported, in any substantial way, by programs or funding from the federal or state governments.

An era of uncertain public funding for community colleges

The last decade of the twentieth century and the first of the twenty-first century were a period of significant change for states as they attempted to manage and fund an increasingly complex range of higher education programs and services. Providing a comprehensive account of this era of change is beyond the scope of this work. But a general description of key developments helps outline the relevancy of the change with respect to community colleges and their students.

To begin with, state funding for community colleges has increased in absolute terms over the past 20 years. But these state revenues are now covering a smaller share of institutions' total operating budgets. As I mentioned earlier, in 1988, about 58 percent of the funding for community colleges was provided by the states. By 2008, only 30 percent of community college operating budgets was provided by the states. This relative decline in state funding has been precipitated by several factors. First, substantial increases in states' expenditures for Medicaid and corrections have resulted in a tightening of state budgets. Because expenses for health care and incarceration are difficult to predict and contain, controlling these expenditures has been an especially difficult problem for the states. Second, over the last 20 years, the enactment of tax and expenditure limitations (TELs) in approximately 30 states, although of questionable effectiveness, has reduced the funds available for higher education in some jurisdictions (New 2010). Perhaps more importantly, these TELs provide some evidence for the public's declining support for higher education, given the other financial demands that taxpayers must endure. Third, and most recently, 34 out of 50 states reported a decrease in state fiscal support for higher education during the Financial Crisis of 2007–08 and the Great Recession of 2007–09 (The Grapevine 2013).

The curtailment of state funding for community colleges has been offset to some extent by significant growth in federal student financial aid and some historical perspective is required in order to appreciate the magnitude of this change. In 1963, before the enactment of the Higher Education Act in 1965, total federal financial aid for undergraduate students was approximately $200 million and this amounted to approximately 36 percent of all undergraduate student financial aid ($550 million) (Lewis 1989). By 2008, however, the federal government was providing $86 billion for undergraduate student financial aid and this was 68 percent of the total ($126 billion) (Baum et al. 2009).

Despite this phenomenal growth in federal student financial aid, many students from low-income families still face substantial hurdles and there are two primary reasons for this. First, as I noted, although federal student financial aid (specifically in the area of loans) was initially focused on helping students with demonstrated financial need, most of these resources are now also available to students from middle and upper class families and this reduces the potential for focusing on the needs of low-income students. Second, the growth of median household income has been stagnant for 30 years (Mishel et al. 2012). This has also had devastating consequences for low-income students attempting to cover their higher education expenses.

Looking ahead, the future of federal student financial aid is now a troubling concern for community college leaders for another reason. The federal government's inability to control expenditures or raise revenue is leading the Congress to scrutinize federal programs more than ever before. In the case of student financial aid, lawmakers are placing new restrictions on these programs to control costs. For instance, the recent revision of the need-based Pell Grant program imposed a new limitation on students' eligibility for support. Now students are limited to 6 years of full-time support. For many students, this revision may not impose a hardship. But for low-income and underprepared students who must return to college to acquire new work skills after being laid off, the unavailability of Pell Grant funding could pose a severe hardship. Researchers are already predicting that this revision will eventually prevent some students from continuing their progress toward completion (Katsinas, Davis, Friedel, Koh, and Grant, 2013). Of course, this development could have cascading negative consequences for the many community colleges that receive state funding based on student enrollment or completion.

The funding problems described above have imposed significant challenges for community colleges and there is every indication they will continue. However, community college leaders were faced with a new set of problems with the arrival of the Financial Crisis of 2007–08 and the Great Recession of 2007–09. Not only did they face the threat of reduced funding from the states and an immediate increase in enrollment, both of which placed new stresses on institutions, but their students encountered even greater challenges in their competition for jobs. And, of course, those students leaving the community college without a credential are in an even worse position when seeking employment.

Reclaiming the American Dream

In April 2012, AACC released another milestone report that made recommendations for the future of community college education. This report was the product of the Twenty-first Century Commission, a panel of community college leaders, university researchers, and policy analysts. In *Reclaiming the*

American Dream, the Twenty-first Century Commission followed a line of argument endorsed by Completion Agenda advocates. The authors observed that the nation was facing two serious problems. First, they noted, "the United States, which for generations led the world in college degree completion, now ranks 16th in the world in completion rates for 25- to 34-year-olds" (AACC 2012, p. viii). Because educational attainment is closely related to economic competitiveness, the failure to produce a sufficient number of college graduates was viewed as a factor contributing toward lower economic growth and higher unemployment. Second, *Reclaiming the American Dream* asserted that the nation had been "underproducing graduates with postsecondary skills since at least 1980" and this was "contributing substantially to income inequality" (AACC 2012, p. viii).

Given these conditions, *Reclaiming the American Dream* proposed a "framework for change" to improve completion rates (AACC 2012, p. ix). This framework included a recommendation that state legislatures adopt a new funding model for community colleges that would prioritize completion instead of enrollment. Also, the proposed framework recommended that public schools make the reforms needed to improve the college readiness of their graduates. Unlike the *Building Communities* report, therefore, the authors of *Reclaiming the American Dream* clearly indicated that others would also need to make substantial changes in order to accomplish the nation's goal of producing more college graduates. Partnerships and closer collaboration would not be sufficient.

The most important dimension of this framework concerned changes that needed to be made at community colleges. *Reclaiming the American Dream* identified two categories of change. The first included changes in how community colleges operated. The second concerned changes in the institution's organizational culture. For example, in the first category, in order to concentrate institutional resources to achieve the greatest positive impact, the Twenty-first Century Commission recommended that public 2-year colleges (a) establish clear, streamlined pathways through curricula to enhance completion, (b) scrutinize the need for expensive "boutique programs," and (c) increase the use of learning analytics to assess student learning. These recommendations were specific and directive. The nation's largest advocacy group for community colleges was now telling college presidents and governing boards that they needed to take concrete steps to produce more completers.

With respect to the second category, in order to ensure alignment of purpose across the institution, *Reclaiming the American Dream* recommended that community colleges take concrete steps to (a) develop a culture of collaboration, (b) decrease the role of faculty prerogative in the instructional process, (c) change the institution's focus from one centered on access to a new focus on access and student success, (d) emphasize student learning instead of faculty teaching, and (e) make decisions based on evidence instead of anecdote. These steps, although not tied to specific programs and services, called upon college leaders to change the way community college employees interact with one another and also with their students.

Reclaiming the American Dream was both an indictment and a roadmap. It described in clear and stark terms the dangers the nation faced if the number of college graduates did not increase. The report acknowledged that community colleges had not been as effective as they could be in preparing students for later life. But the Twenty-first Century Commission proclaimed, if community colleges were willing to adopt a new vision that focused on access *and* completion, positive change would happen.

Reclaiming the American Dream did not include any rhetoric about building communities. There was no discussion of growing outward "from a core of integrity and confidence" (AACC 1988, p. 49). And there was no mention of grounding change on "humane goals" (AACC 1988, p. 49). The dominant theme throughout the report was that community colleges needed to advance the Completion Agenda. And the values and priorities behind the Completion Agenda were unabashedly guided by an economic logic emphasizing the importance of national economic growth, lower unemployment, and arresting the rise in income inequality. Finally, as any reader of *Reclaiming the American Dream* would see, the report claimed that community colleges had an important responsibility to secure the American democracy. But the authors declined to say precisely what they meant by democracy or how it might be advanced. And references to democracy consistently placed it in a position subordinate to economic growth.

Conclusion

The evolution of community colleges in the 1940s and 1950s aligned with the aspirations of a nation emerging from a world war with Fascism in Europe and Asia. The GI Bill and the Truman Commission Report advocated an expansion of educational opportunity for adults and community colleges played a central role in pursuing this goal. What soon became evident, however, was that community colleges would also play a role in advancing the nation's other higher education priorities. Clark and then Brint and Karabel found that junior colleges and community colleges did something more than provide adult learners with educational opportunity. They also carried out a critical sorting process that ensured only best-prepared students would go to university study and then the most desirable careers. This sorting worked well for community colleges, universities, employers, and the society. But, as Clark reported, it deceptively moved students into vocational curricula that usually led to blue-collar jobs.

The phenomenal enrollment growth during the boom years of the 1960s and 1970s solidified the community college role in American higher education. And this growth was due to strong direct support from the state governments (institutional appropriations) and strong indirect support from the federal government (student financial aid). But, beginning in the 1990s, state governments encountered a series of problems that led them to curtail growth in funding for higher education and community colleges. The rise in state expenditures for Medicaid and corrections, the increasing popularity of TELs, and finally the Financial Crisis of 2007–08 and the Great Recession of 2007–09 all eventually led to reduced state funding for community colleges. After 20 years, it was clear, the change was dramatic. The states provided 58 percent of the funding for community colleges in 1988, but this fell to 30 percent by 2008.

In response to the fraying social fabric of the 1980s, in 1988, AACC released *Building Communities*, which recommended that community colleges also take on the responsibility of community development. The impact of the report is difficult to assess and it advocated a role that, although important, was not effectively supported by the federal and state governments. Unfortunately, the trends that contributed to this decline (limited economic growth, increasing income inequality, and a loss of a sense of community) continued for the next 12 years. The chances for recovery during the first decade of the twenty-first century evaporated after the terrorist attacks of September 11, 2001 and the diversion of trillions of dollars into overseas wars. The permanent political stalemate that overshadowed the federal government scuttled any chance of developing some political and social consensus on how the nation should deal with these social and economic problems.

Looking back over the last 35 years, we see that the normative vision that guided community colleges was one that prioritized the expansion of educational opportunity. In this respect the evolution of community colleges aligned with the 1964 Civil Rights Act and the 1965 Higher Education Act. In the 1988 report, *Building Communities*, the Commission on the Future of Community Colleges recommended a vision for the twenty-first century that continued to stress educational opportunity. The report also affirmed the values of diversity, collaboration, service, participation, effective teaching, and lifelong learning. But *Building Communities* also called upon community colleges to help build communities. The overarching vision of a community college committed to access and building community appealed to the hearts of community college leaders, but not to the minds of federal and state politicians.

In the 2012 report, *Reclaiming the American Dream*, another AACC special commission reframed the vision for community colleges and argued that community colleges needed to commit themselves to access *and* completion. *Reclaiming the American Dream* argued that community colleges, guided by a new vision of access and completion, could play a vital role in resolving the nation's great problems—limited economic growth and increasing inequality. The fundamental premise of *Reclaiming the American Dream*, therefore, was that the American Dream could be reclaimed through an improved economy. This line of thinking avoided any serious consideration of the problems identified in the 1988 *Building Communities* report, that is, the erosion of the ethical values and human relations in American communities. Yet, as the Truman Commission noted in 1947, these ethical values and human relations—not the economy—were the foundation of American democracy.

PART THREE

Dewey on education, democracy, and community

8

The relationship between democracy and education

Introduction

Two broad considerations justify examining the work of John Dewey in a search for a new normative vision for American community colleges. First, over the last 25 years, discussion about the vision for the future of community college education has been contradictory. The *Building Communities* report advocated for an educational institution distinguished by a more collaborative culture on campus, the pursuit of more humane goals, and closer cooperation with off-campus partners. The authors of *Building Communities* specifically declined to endorse a more market-focused approach for a normative vision. In 2012, *Reclaiming the American Dream* advocated for educational priorities that aligned with national economic policy. Clearly, there are very different and competing visions for the future of community college education. The conversation about the future of community college education remains very much alive and open. And, given the great social and economic challenges of the day, this is the time to consider other visions to guide the evolution of community colleges.

Second, as I explained in Chapter 4, there is much we can learn from John Dewey, an American who thought carefully about the relationship between education and democracy during an era that in many respects is similar to our own. In this chapter, therefore, I sketch out Dewey's early work on education and democracy and start to show how his insights may be helpful in developing a new normative vision for community colleges.

The context for *Democracy and Education*

Dewey's *Democracy and Education*, published in 1916, explained his views on education and its relationship to democracy (Dewey 2008/1916, "Democracy and Education"). Dewey's discussion in the book was grounded in his formal training and study as a philosopher. He acknowledged and then responded to the educational theories of modern and ancient philosophers such as Spencer and Plato. But the book was most influenced by his life experiences. *Democracy and Education* was the product, therefore, of a man writing in his late 50s, who had learned from his observations of the Pullman Strike and the struggles of poor immigrants working in Chicago's dangerous slaughterhouses. He had experienced the loss of two children, perhaps the most unpredictable and cruel of personal tragedies. He had also witnessed scientific advancements, the rapid pace of industrialization, and its transformation of social life. *Democracy and Education* was also informed, however, by Dewey's close monitoring of overseas developments in Europe during the early years of World War I, 1914 and 1915.

During the first decade of the twentieth century, Dewey, like many academics, regarded Germany, led by Kaiser Wilhelm II, as one of the world's most advanced nations, leading in science, industry, commerce, and education (Brose 2010; Letter from John Dewey to George Stuart Fullerton, December 4, 1914 (03265)). The German university was the model guiding the development of American universities. German professors had won top international prizes for their accomplishments in basic research, especially in chemistry and physics. Many educated Americans, therefore, looked upon Germany with admiration even though it had not made the transition to a modern political democracy.

By 1915, however, Americans viewed Germany as the nation primarily responsible for the war and Kaiser Wilhelm II as the reckless Emperor who had forced the conflict in order to show the world he was a great leader. The magnitude of this error and the resulting war damage are difficult to fathom today. World War I would eventually cost the lives of almost 10 million soldiers, with another 20 million wounded, and 7 million missing. As for material losses, by the end of the conflict in 1918, several of the great European powers would be bankrupted and their empires broken up and distributed as spoils of war. These consequences had not yet played out when Dewey wrote *Democracy and Education*. But, growing up in a country wracked by civil war, he surely knew, as many others did too, that the ultimate cost of the war could be astronomical.

In *Democracy and Education*, therefore, Dewey explained that an effective educational system was essential to the development of a more intelligent people and a more just society. But such a system was also a prerequisite to the creation of a society which had at least some advantage, he believed, in avoiding the tragic military conflict into which Europe's great monarchies had blundered. When writing about education, Dewey was an optimist. He had a deep faith in our ability to grow and construct a better democracy. But he also knew that human life was fragile and that societies could easily fall into ruin for any number of reasons. Effective educational systems, therefore, provided the means to develop an intelligent populace that could select wise leaders capable of avoiding the errors often made by those who held political power as a result of ancestry or marriage.

Defining democracy

Dewey wrote *Democracy and Education* as a classroom text to help prepare teachers. Each chapter was well organized. Each closed with a summary that made study of the text easier. The overriding purpose of the book was to identify and explain the kind of education needed to promote individual growth and the American democracy. Teachers had a big responsibility when they were assigned to teach science or mathematics or history. What was even more important, however, was the work they did in helping students develop the intelligence, habits, and character needed to secure a modern democracy.

One of the early topics Dewey addressed was the conventional understanding of democracy. He observed that traditionally, American school children were taught that democracy was a form of government. Indeed, most Americans believed their democracy was a consequence of the American Revolution when the colonists rejected the rule of the British monarchy and, after adopting a written constitution, established their own representative government. But, Dewey argued, much more was involved in creating the American democracy.

For Dewey, the historical record was clear on this point. The American democracy had improved a great deal since the late-eighteenth century. People enjoyed more freedom and opportunities. Slavery had been abolished and women were gaining equal rights. But the changes in the law correcting these injustices were the consequence of social movements and years of intense struggle that played out not just in political venues but in social and economic settings as well. To be sure, the shorthand explanation of these changes was that unjust laws were repealed. But this was a simplistic explanation for what were, in fact, very complex developments.

When Dewey examined the historical record, he found that the real catalysts for these great changes were the scientific and technological advancements that changed the way people lived (e.g., the production of electricity, the invention of the steam engine and the telegraph). As improvements in communication and transportation enabled more people to travel and share information, they learned more about one another and their society. This deeper understanding of people and human society is what led to a change in

Americans' beliefs about slavery and women's rights. And this is what led to the repeal of unjust laws.

Dewey noted that Americans have always had an almost religious reverence for the democratic institutions and legal rights created by the US Constitution. But this glorification of the past usually did more harm than good. It exaggerated the merit of past social and economic arrangements secured by these institutions and legal rights. It also discounted the severity of contemporary social and economic injustices that remained legal under these institutions and legal rights.

Dewey accepted that a representative form of government and fundamental legal rights were a necessary part of a democracy. But they were not sufficient. When he looked back over the course of American history, he saw that "a democracy is more than a form of government; it is primarily a mode of associated living, of conjoint communicated experience" (Dewey 2008/1916, "Democracy and Education," p. 93). And, he observed, associated living in a democracy is marked by two features. First, members of the society have "more numerous and more varied points of shared common interest" (Dewey 2008/1916, "Democracy and Education," p. 93). Second, there is "freer interaction between social groups" (Dewey 2008/1916, "Democracy and Education," p. 93). What Dewey found was that a gradual increase in freer interaction and the development of shared common interests best explained why Americans eventually recognized the injustices in their society and then forced the legal and political systems to correct them. These circumstances best explained why democracy had developed in the United States. For Dewey, therefore, democracy was much more than a form of government. It was a way of life.

Because change in a democracy was usually guided by the people, as a result of debate and dialogue, democratic societies had a vital interest in preparing citizens to do this work. Accordingly, Dewey wrote, a democracy had a great interest in providing everyone with access to "deliberate and systematic education" (Dewey 2008/1916, "Democracy and Education," p. 93). In a monarchy or oligarchy, the balance between social stability and social change is orchestrated from above. If necessary, these societies can maintain stability or promote change through authoritarian measures such as surveillance, administrative detention, exile, and criminal prosecution. In a democracy, however, social stability is ultimately acquired through deliberate and systematic education. An educational system that is deliberate and systematic provides all members of the society with the capacity (i.e., the skills, the dispositions, and the values) to resolve problems.

Dewey also observed that in the past, societies tended to be mono-cultural. The people in a dominant class, race, or religion usually defined the values of a society and controlled the power structure to ensure respect for these values. Modern societies, however, were much more complex. There are, Dewey noted, "not only political subdivisions, but industrial, scientific, religious, associations. There are political parties with differing aims, social sets, cliques, gangs, corporations, partnerships, groups bound closely together by ties of blood, and so in endless variety" (Dewey 2008/1916, "Democracy and Education," p. 87). And, "in many modern states," Dewey added, "there is great diversity of populations, of varying languages, religions, moral codes, and traditions" (Dewey 2008/1916, "Democracy and Education," p. 87). In a healthy and stable democracy, this diversity became a strength. People in one community reached out to understand their counterparts in a different community and through their interaction gained new knowledge and developed common interests. These common interests, in turn provided the basis for growth and collaboration in ways that resulted in outcomes desirable to both communities. Again, however, this kind of growth and collaboration required an educational system that provided people with the capacity to interact with others to solve problems.

Dewey realized, of course, that any modern society, even a democracy, could be adversely affected by technological advancements and new social and economic conditions. Throughout his life, he lamented the development of technologies, habits, and customs that contributed to individual isolation. When people were isolated within their own communities, their knowledge of others was always mediated by the media and this inevitably obstructed the development of shared understandings. This isolation often divided people and obscured injustices perpetuated by class privilege and racial discrimination. An effective educational system provided young people with the capacity and motivation to solve problems and facilitate the development of democratic communities. Yes, he agreed, democratic political institutions and fundamental rights were essential. But, for him, the more important indicator of a democracy was when people developed and maintained a *democratic culture*.

Learning in a democratic community

Dewey's training and experience led him to see that learning was a social process and this was the case whether it occurred in a democracy or in some other society. He acknowledged that in some cases facts or skills could be learned in isolation. But for Dewey, the meaning and relevancy of these facts or skills could only be learned socially. It was only in social settings that a child or adult could learn how a particular fact or learned behavior related to a larger task, to an occupation, to a business, or to the community.

Dewey also recognized that learning and growth were not limited by a person's age. Yes, children and adults learned different things and in different ways. But learning was a natural state for humans and they retained a capacity to learn unless it was driven out of them. Children had a natural curiosity and plasticity that made them receptive to learning. With proper encouragement, this curiosity and plasticity could facilitate the development of good habits that would lead to a disposition to learn and grow. Unfortunately, this disposition in adults was often diminished. Still, he argued, so long as adults lived in encouraging communities, growth and learning remained not only possible but a natural quality of human life.

Dewey contended that the central purpose of education was to help children and adults live more intentionally. By this, he meant that an education should help people gain a deeper understanding of their experience so they could make the adjustments necessary to better understand their present circumstances and thereby gain greater control over their lives in the future. For Dewey, a person could live more intentionally in two ways.

In what he referred to as static societies, people learned in order to enjoy experiences or achieve goals validated by the status quo. In a democracy, however, people learned in order to develop better habits and dispositions that will help create a better society. In a democracy, the purpose of educational systems was not to secure the status quo or to help people conform to some ideal. Their purpose was to provide children and adults with the skills, values, and dispositions needed to effectively address the problems immediately before them. After a person had studied a problem in collaboration with others, he could reflect on their shared experience, learn from it, and use it to gain better control over the future. For Dewey, learning in schools or colleges was best advanced through shared problem solving. But learning in these institutions entailed a significant moral responsibility as well. For Dewey, the moral duty assigned to schools and colleges was not to punish or threaten students as a means to encourage learning but to help them develop into effective citizens capable of sustaining and advancing a democratic society.

Dewey maintained that the first responsibility of educators in developing learning objectives was to ensure that they promote individual growth and the development of democratic communities. Good objectives had three characteristics. First, they were based on real problems. Second, they were flexible so students and teachers could revise them to accommodate changes in the problem under study. Third, good educational aims encouraged students to focus not on the "correct answer" or some specific outcome but on the unique aspects of the problem under study. Dewey's experience in the classroom showed him that when students were guided by good aims and actively participated in solving a problem, they remembered the problem and their solutions to it. They also developed the habits and dispositions that prepared them for active, problem-solving collaboration with others. On the other hand, when students were directed to complete assignments or tests in isolation, in a rote manner, they took on the role of spectators and mimics, simply watching and then replicating the behaviors they observed in their instructor. Students subjected to this regime had little hope of experiencing individual growth, developing an understanding of life's problems, or accepting responsibility for improving themselves or their society.

Dewey's discussion of educational aims shows us how he envisioned learning in a democracy. He understood that education must be much more than preparation for a career or demonstrating mastery of a set of competencies. A critical objective of effective education in a democracy was individual growth. And growth needed to be based on the students' experience and not some conceptual model dictated by an instructor. As Dewey stated, to accomplish genuine learning, "An ounce of experience is better than a ton of theory" (Dewey 2008/1916, "Democracy and Education," p. 151).

Good instructors also needed to help students understand the social dimensions of their studies and this called for the development of a "social spirit" in educational institutions (Dewey 2008/1916, "Democracy and Education," p. 368). An educational institution with a social spirit had two qualities. First, the institution was a community in all respects. Second, learning was framed by the experiences students had in their community. What Dewey was telling educators here was that schools would only be effective in supporting the development of a democracy if they made a concern for students' lives and the community, high priorities. Once a school or college succeeded in developing this social spirit, this sense of democratic morality, it could serve as a transformative institution in the community. Only then would students take responsibility for their own growth, the growth of their classmates, and develop the capacity to help solve problems in the community. This was the path to a democracy and, as Dewey noted, following it required educational institutions committed as intensely to individual growth and the development of democratic communities as to the subjects taught in the curriculum.

Preparing people for work in a democratic community

Vocational education was another theme addressed in *Democracy and Education*. Dewey's discussion of the topic was spurred by the rapid growth of vocational education curricula in public schools during the late nineteenth and early twentieth centuries. But he also addressed the subject because vocational education programs were used to perniciously track students into different career paths. Children from working poor and immigrant families were often diverted into these programs because they were viewed as genetically inclined for manual labor. However, students from middle and upper class families were usually prepared for high school and perhaps college because of the belief that they were naturally more intelligent. Dewey strongly opposed the use of vocational education programs as a device to replicate the existing class structure. But he was not opposed to preparing people for work. This was an essential part of any education.

In a democracy, educational institutions needed to prepare people for "an occupation." But, for him, an occupation meant something more than a job or a career or a static set of skills. He used the term "occupation" to refer to a continuing focus or purpose in life that brought satisfaction and meaning to the individual and benefits to the society. When he wrote about occupations he referred to the life of a scientist or gardener or artist. To find satisfaction and meaning in any of these occupations required a course of preparation that did much more than teach work skills. It required providing students with an understanding of the occupation's history and relevancy to the society. This more holistic and contextual approach would require a radically new and different system of education. Such a system required,

> instruction in the historic background of present conditions; . . . study of economics, civics, and politics, to bring the future worker into touch with the problems of the day and the various methods proposed for its improvement. Above all, it would train power of readaptation to changing conditions so that future workers would not become blindly subject to a fate imposed upon them. (Dewey 2008/1916, "Democracy and Education," p. 328)

Dewey's call for a more holistic and contextual foundation for vocational education was not driven by a desire to provide students with a more theoretical understanding of their work. On the contrary, he was motivated by very practical concerns. He understood that whether a person worked in executive offices or on a factory floor, he would be working in a hierarchical organization. Satisfactory employment in such an organization would require an understanding of its cultural, social, and economic dimensions so people could survive in it and successfully negotiate employment, promotions, and other workplace changes.

Dewey also stressed that "the only adequate training *for* occupations is training *through* occupations" (Dewey 2008/1916, "Democracy and Education," p. 320, emphasis in the original). For him, good, relevant hands-on experiences were an essential component of any school or college curriculum. Consequently, he had a special scorn for the traditional curriculum offered at many private academies that provided privileged students with an education in the classics and little more. This only prepared students for a life of privilege and leisure and in most cases little social benefit would come from this kind of education.

Finally, Dewey claimed that preparation for an occupation could happen throughout a person's life. He understood that people would settle on an occupation at different times or they might move from one occupation to another to adapt to changing circumstances. We tend to think of our own era as unique and one where people are often required to move from one workplace to the next in order to stay employed. But, at the turn of the twentieth century, when many Americans were migrating from rural to urban areas, without employment services or unemployment insurance, the challenges of remaining employed were even more difficult. Dewey recognized these challenges and understood that even after students graduated from high school or college, many would need to return from time to time for further education. In a society committed to individual growth and the development of democratic communities, educational institutions would need to serve people of all ages and at all points in their life to ensure they could continue to grow and lead happy and productive lives.

Conclusion

At this point it may be helpful to restate the qualities or values of effective and deliberate educational systems that Dewey identified as necessary to sustain and advance democracy. First, these educational systems needed to be accessible to all. Second, they needed to support individual growth and the development of democratic communities. Third, students needed to be taught to become more intentional by reflecting on their experience and learning from this to gain more control over their lives. Fourth, these educational systems must help students develop the skills, values, and dispositions needed to work together with people from diverse communities to solve problems. Fifth, they must prepare students for an occupation, a life activity that would bring personal satisfaction but also some benefit to the community. And, finally, these educational systems needed to be available to people throughout their lives to ensure their continued satisfaction or capacity to contribute to the society. Dewey was concerned, therefore, with both the means and ends of education and their influence on democracy.

Dewey recognized, of course, that the American system of education was not created to help people grow and develop their democracy. It was designed and operated to reproduce the status quo; an arrangement of political, economic, and social conditions that isolated people, and secured the privileges granted by class, race, and gender. Still, even with this understanding,

Dewey was an optimist and his life experiences convinced him that progress was not only possible but probable. Dewey regarded effective and deliberate educational systems as having the capacity to transform a community but also, when taken to scale, as having the capacity to transform the society. The transformation Dewey thought of, however, was not targeted on some predetermined arrangement of political, social, and economic conditions. He was much too practical to believe in a human utopia. But, with continued advancements in science and technology, a transformation to a more just and equitable society was possible. And this kind of change was well within the capacity of effective and deliberate educational systems.

9

The Great Society and the Great Community

Introduction

In *Democracy and Education* Dewey described and explained a democracy as a way of life and explained what educational systems must do to strengthen and secure this way of life. Once readers understood that a democracy was much more than a political system, they could begin to see why schools were essential in educating people for life in such a society. Although anyone could learn a great deal outside of formal education, institutions were needed to help learners critically reflect on their experience, understand the lives of others, and then synthesize their insights with their classmates. From 1916 to the late 1920s Dewey's work on democracy began to move away from a description and explanation of democracy to a more finely tuned investigation of (a) the individual and social conditions that impeded the development of democracies and (b) the essential conditions of a specific kind of democracy, that is, the Great Community.

His writings during this era were informed by his experiences in traveling internationally for extended periods of time. They were also motivated by debates he had with others about the state of the American democracy. Dewey's account of the problems facing the American democracy was not unique. But his description of the solutions to these problems was. He argued that the solutions lay outside the scope of government and concerned the ways people lived in their communities. The solutions, in other words, were not ultimately matters of government policy or practice. Dewey's proposals left his readers with a heavy responsibility. There was no government office or tax policy or social program that would fix the American democracy. The commitment to democracy would need to be made by individuals and it would need to run throughout all aspects of their lives, day after day. Dewey knew, like many others, that Americans had a history of rising to the occasion when faced with national or international crises. Americans would step up. They would even sacrifice their lives if required. But, absent a sense of urgency, they usually accepted the status quo. Dewey understood this. Consequently in the writings reviewed here he argued that the only way to focus on long-term individual growth and development of democratic communities was to establish effective and deliberate educational systems and identify and resolve the individual and social problems that compromised the education of the public. Without this focus and commitment, the evolution of the American democracy would become vulnerable to internal and external threats.

Social divisions and universal education

After the United States entered World War I in 1917, New York City's port facilities were very busy shipping men and armaments off to Great Britain and the Western front in France and Belgium. These activities were reported in the nation's newspapers. Along with many others, Dewey began to wonder what else the nation might accomplish if Americans made the same kind of effort to tackle social problems at home. This was not an abstract musing for Dewey. At the time, many Americans believed the country was facing serious internal threats such as "social disorder and confusion and conflict" (Dewey 2008/1918, "Vocational Education in the Light of the World War," p. 68). The United States had deep divisions between the classes and many were frustrated that wealthy families failed to understand the magnitude of their privilege. Their children attended private academies and boarding schools and were often isolated and kept away from the extreme poverty found in many immigrant and working poor neighborhoods. Also, children from immigrant and working poor families did not receive an education that provided them the capacity to participate effectively in the political system. He expressed these concerns in a 1916 essay published in the *New Republic*, where he wrote,

> Speaking roughly, our youth of the more favored class have much done for them, and little is expected in return; there is little to foster public-mindedness. Politically they are spoiled children. The less favored youth are so preoccupied with the practical demands of the moment and the relaxations of sparse moments of relief, that the state is for them also a remote and pallid entity. Our easygoing disposition, our comfort, our size, our congested towns, the invitations of the passing hour, combine with our individualistic tradition to depress from view the claims of organized society. We are over stimulated in matters of personal success and enjoyment;

we have little that teaches subordination to the public good or that secures effective capacity to work cooperatively in its behalf. (Dewey 2008/1916, "Universal Service as Education," p. 187)

Along with Dewey, thoughtful adults from both rich and poor families realized that growing inequality in income and wealth was eroding the moral fabric of the community. Accordingly, many Americans began to think more earnestly of how their society could be improved, and more specifically, how the gap between rich and poor could be reduced.

Some argued for compulsory military service as a way to integrate immigrants and other "social outcasts" into a new American "melting-pot" (Dewey 2008/1916, "Universal Service as Education," p. 184). Dewey saw this as an ineffective way to integrate newcomers and one that would not respect the traditional beliefs and cultures of their communities. Instead, he called for greater federal support for the public schools so they could educate more children, especially those of immigrant parents. In 1916, he argued that a major investment of federal funds, to support public education, was just as important as the expenditures being made on men and armaments to fight the war overseas.

When World War I ended in 1918, Dewey renewed his call for change in how the nation educated its young people. He argued for a fundamental reconstruction and reorganization of education. And, he added, "it must go on with a view of greater liberation of human power" (Dewey 2008/1918, "Vocational Education in Light of the World War," p. 60). This could be accomplished, Dewey wrote, by implementing a new form of universal education for older youth, emphasizing the importance of social service and service to the community. Such a reformation of American education would be comparable to the European form of universal military service required for young men (Dewey 2008/1918, "Vocational Education in Light of the World War"). The schools would enroll young men and young women, it would be vocational in a Deweyan sense where students would be educated in an occupation, and graduates would be prepared to make some contribution to the society. This new form of universal education would include intellectual and physical education along with public health education since it was clear, he noted, that the nation's overall health was being undermined by substance abuse (alcoholism), poor sanitation, and diseases associated with poverty. Finally, this system of universal education would also instruct students in "methods of industrial management and operation which will promote civic efficiency and the cooperative spirit" (Dewey 2008/1918, "Vocational Education in Light of the World War," p. 64).

Dewey acknowledged that his proposal was only "an outline in very broad features on a very broad canvas" (Dewey 2008/1918, "Vocational Education in

Light of the World War," p. 66). But, if implemented, it would be an important step toward strengthening the nation's democracy and addressing its great social divisions. And, he believed, this would offer something more than the *ad hoc* development of junior college programs which were sprouting up across the country. As he stated, "The problem is not one of adding things on to the present high school. It is a problem of thoroughgoing reconstruction" (Dewey 2008/1918. "The Problem of Secondary Education," p. 28). Many administrative details were left unaddressed, matters that seldom stopped Dewey from pointing toward a better future. But his proposal did explain how the nation could utilize the great sense of social purpose and national courage mustered to fight World War I and then continue development of American democracy while addressing serious social problems at home.

In January 1919, Dewey left for Japan where he delivered a series of lectures at the Imperial University in Tokyo in February and March (Dykhuizen 1973). Dewey's lectures became a first draft of *Reconstruction in Philosophy*, a short, pithy book that summarized his pragmatic philosophy and then explained its location in the history of Western philosophy (Ross, "Introduction," 2008). After concluding his work in Japan, he toured the country and then left for China in late April. Dewey had not planned for an extended stay in China but his visit lasted almost 2 and ½ years.

The role of habits, dispositions, and customs

After returning from China in the summer of 1921, Dewey resumed his teaching and writing at Columbia and soon his new book, *Human Nature and Conduct*, was out in print. In this book he argued that understanding human behavior was not possible unless we could discern how it was influenced by social and economic conditions. It followed, therefore, that improving human behavior in an intelligent, humane, and constructive manner inevitably required that we change the social and economic conditions that serve as the context for it. This view countered the widespread belief in the academy that the key to understanding human behavior lay in a close analysis of specific human acts studied in isolation.

The central concept in Dewey's discussion was habit. His notion of habit varied significantly from the common understanding which regarded habit as some form of repetitive or recurring behavior. For Dewey, a habit was, "an acquired predisposition to *ways* or modes of response, . . . standing predilections and aversions, rather than bare recurrence of specific acts" (Dewey 2008/1922, "Human Nature and Conduct, p. 32, emphasis in the original). This explanation pushed readers to recognize that a habit entailed much more than just behavior. The habit of intelligent thought, for example, was demonstrated in a person's attentive, careful, systematic, and courageous analysis of a problem. Intelligent thought was also exhibited in a person's sustained efforts over time to consider a problem in its proper context, free of distractions, prejudices, and biases to the extent these were known. Good habits led to the formation of good dispositions. And, considered collectively over time, these would lead to the formation of constructive social customs.

Dewey's conceptualization of human habit explained how people formed and then adhered to complex predispositions. It also explained how these dispositions led to and secured social and cultural customs. Once we understood the relationship between habits, dispositions, and customs, we could begin to see why people ignore evidence and rational arguments and, through the force of habit, hold on to irrational or outdated beliefs about humans and society.

Putting the issue in a positive light, Dewey argued that if educators understood the role of habits they could help students develop a reflective disposition which could in turn lead to constructive social and cultural customs. A finely tuned reflective disposition, focused on the advancement of democracy was, perhaps, the most important disposition that students could develop in school. And contrary to social critics, like Walter Lippmann, who believed the masses were hopelessly limited in their ability to think reflectively, Dewey argued that this was entirely possible. As he explained, "The reflective disposition is not self-made nor a gift of the gods" (Dewey 2008/1922, "Human Nature and Conduct, p. 56, emphasis in the original). The ability to critically reflect on social and economic circumstances was something that could be developed in a generation of students and then lead to significant positive social change.

Dewey's optimism about the potential for positive social change ran throughout *Human Nature and Conduct*. But he was not naïve. A more intelligent understanding of human behavior only offered the potential of developing a society more receptive to democracy. It was a necessary condition for developing a democracy, not sufficient in itself. Hopefully, over time, the development of a new reflective disposition throughout the community would enable people to form new social customs and change the institutions impeding the advancement of democratic culture. In Dewey's view, the work would take time. But there was no other effective path to social progress. Some might advocate for a more immediate and even violent path to change. But Dewey rejected violence as a method to accomplish social change.

When *Human Nature and Conduct* was published in 1922, Dewey was 63 years old. He had accomplished enough to justify a slower pace in his work. But instead, over the next 5 years, he traveled widely, read widely, and focused more intently on political philosophy. Invitations to lecture again led him to travel across the United States and also to tour Germany and Turkey in 1924; France, Spain, Austria, Denmark, Sweden, and Great Britain in 1925. Dewey encountered tragedy again, however, when his wife Alice suffered declining health as a result of malaria contracted in 1925 and then died in New York in July 1927, following complications from arteriosclerosis.

Lippmann's critique of the American democracy

Over the course of Dewey's long career, he debated many issues with philosophers, social scientists, and public commentators. Most of these debates were played out on the pages of magazines, journals, and books. In the field of political philosophy, Dewey's greatest debate was in the 1920s, when he entered into an extended discussion with Walter Lippmann. Lippmann was born in 1889 and was 30 years younger than Dewey. Lippmann studied philosophy at Harvard University and graduated in 1910 (Goodwin 1995; Luskin 1972; Steel 1980). After leaving college, he became a journalist. He was the founding editor of the *New Republic*, a Pulitzer Prize-winning newspaper columnist, and before he died at the age of 85 in 1974, had authored more than a dozen books on American politics and American foreign policy.

Lippmann's bestselling 1922 book, *Public Opinion*, made two bold claims about the American democracy. First, he politely, but firmly, explained why the common man was incapable of making good decisions about important public policy issues. Second, he argued that a well-educated, open-minded elite, committed to using the scientific method, might be the only group capable of solving the great problems facing the American democracy (Lippmann 1922). In *Public Opinion*, Lippmann began his argument by asserting that people only understand their social world through fictions. These fictions were not lies. But they were representations people created to explain a society that was far too complicated to be completely understood. As Lippmann wrote,

> the real environment is altogether too big, too complex, and too fleeting for direct acquaintance. We are not equipped to deal with so much subtlety, so much variety, so many permutations and combinations. . . . To traverse the world men must have maps of the world. (Lippmann 1922, p. 16)

People create such maps—mental representations of their society—in order to help them make decisions. But these maps could be flawed in two respects. First, they were inevitably limited by external constraints. For example, they were constructed with incomplete and inaccurate information. Second, our knowledge of the world was not just limited by our inability to gather complete and accurate information; it was also limited by the inherent constraints of human consciousness. More specifically, Lippmann contended that when people do access information, they examine it in ways that conform to concepts and processes already believed and validated by their environment and culture.

Lippmann added that because the public is unable to develop a complete and accurate assessment of social problems, its assessment of public policy cannot truly be said to be based on a genuine understanding of the issues. Accordingly, in a representative democracy the public's approval of governmental policy requires the manufacture of consent. Shrewd leaders manufacture consent by creating a compelling narrative that is incomplete or even false. The public, with only limited time and energy to examine the narrative, usually bought it.

Lippmann's description was convincing and many of his readers reluctantly accepted his discouraging diagnosis of American society. He grounded his argument on examples from American political history that were persuasive and timely. For instance, he explained how the American government and its supporters in the media manufactured consent to go to war in 1917 by using negative stereotypes of the German people.

The rationale for Lippmann's critique was not only grounded on the propaganda and events that led the nation into World War I. Understanding the disengaged American public also required a brief history lesson on how the nation had changed since colonial times. Lippmann acknowledged that in the early days of the nation, people in small rural towns often succeeded in resolving the big problems confronting their community. We can imagine how the colonists in New England were able to work together to find new sources for drinking water. They also contributed their labor and materials to build a new school or courthouse. But in the twentieth century and especially in large cities, the problems were much greater. The reality was that modern day citizens (whom Lippmann referred to as "outsiders") were preoccupied by their family, business, and social activities and rarely had the time or energy to collect, analyze, and then interpret information in order to provide intelligent feedback on complex social problems or government policies (Lippmann 1922, p. 388).

Lippman's critique also presented a harsh assessment of the media, the enterprise believed by many to be the best watchdog of government officials. He argued that any faith in the media was seriously misplaced. Newspapers focused on discrete events and did not have the capacity to explain complex issues in a larger social context. Also, newspapers relied upon advertisers for revenue and usually would not print a story if it might offend them. What was needed, he argued, was the organization of an elite class of technical experts to investigate serious social problems and then formulate policy recommendations for the legislative and executive branches of the federal government. Lippmann contended that a series of "intelligence bureaus" aligned with the major departments of the federal government and coordinated by a central agency, could do the work needed to place important issues before elected officials for their consideration (Lippmann 1922, p. 387).

Lippmann's intelligence bureaus would operate in the following manner. First, the professional staff of an intelligence bureau would have authority to collect data, to examine any document or record, and could compel government officials to answer inquiries. Second, in order to preclude political sabotage, the bureaus would have an endowed funding stream that, although ultimately under the control of the Congress, would be resistant to tampering. Third, the professional staff of intelligence bureaus would be tenured for life with dismissal only ordered after a group of competent peers determined there was some serious misdeed. Fourth, in order to encourage collaboration across the bureaus, staff would be required to share their information and findings with their counterparts. Lippmann believed that this kind of government bureaucracy, linked to all the major industries of the country, would lead to more scientific and successful governance. And finally, Lippmann wrote that an important advantage of the intelligence bureaus was that they would help limit the public's attention to issues before they were thoroughly analyzed by the experts.

Dewey reviewed Lippmann's *Public Opinion* in the *New Republic* in the spring of 1922. Dewey agreed that the American democracy was in dire straits and that important policy decisions were being made by political leaders who manufactured the consent of the governed through their manipulation of the media. The solution to this problem, however, was not the expansion of the federal government and the creation of a new government bureaucracy. Dewey rejected the idea that the cure for bad government was more government. Instead, a much better course of action was helping Americans develop new educational systems to ensure that young people acquired the capacity to think critically and reflectively. Once they had this capacity, they could identify their own political and economic interests and then advocate for them. Dewey's review was well received by his readers but it did not deter Lippmann from continuing his discouraging line of argument.

In 1925, Lippmann followed up with another book examining the relationship between the public and its government, *The Phantom Public* (Lippmann 1925, *The Phantom Public*). In this work, Lippmann was even more pessimistic about the potential of outsiders to play a meaningful role in their democracy. He argued that well-informed political leaders (or "insiders" as he called them) had obtained a firm grip on the levers of power and he had little confidence in the ability of citizens to regain control. Lippmann characterized what he viewed as the public's frustratingly short attention span with an analogy that was sharp but on the mark. He wrote, "The public will arrive in the middle of the third act and will leave before the last curtain, having stayed just long enough perhaps to decide who is the hero and who the villain of the piece"(Lippmann, *The Phantom Public*, 1925, p. 65; Steel 1980). Lippmann's cynicism annoyed some of his readers, especially those who saw his youth and intellectual promise undermined by a pessimism more commonly found in older intellectuals. But his conclusion was unequivocal. Lippmann had lost confidence in the ability of Americans to become more engaged and active. He had concluded that powerful interests would continue to buy off government leaders, through legal and illegal means. Perhaps most importantly, he had given up any hope that Americans could recover and still play a meaningful role in their democracy.

Dewey reviewed *The Phantom Public* in the *New Republic* in December 1925 (Dewey 2008/1925, "Practical Democracy"). He acknowledged that insiders were corrupting the nation's political democracy and making decisions that favored the powerful. He agreed that Americans were losing confidence in their government's ability to make decisions advancing the best interests of the nation. But the aging philosopher faced these problems with a more positive outlook. He criticized Lippmann for assuming that the government, and government alone, was capable of making the changes needed to advance democracy. Dewey argued, as he had in the past, that the people retained the capacity to improve their democracy. Dewey's review of *The Phantom Public*, however, was not his last word on the topic.

Creating the Great Community

Dewey's full response to Lippmann was first set out in lectures delivered in January 1926 at Kenyon College in Ohio and then in the publication of these lectures in 1927 in *The Public and Its Problems*. The essential premise of the book was his conviction that the path to a better democracy entailed development of a culture that valued and practised reflective thinking and active collaboration in order to solve the community's problems.

In *The Public and Its Problems*, Dewey agreed with Lippmann's claim that in the 1920s the American public was largely ineffective in exerting any significant influence on the government. Dewey attributed this circumstance to two conditions. First, most people in the society were apathetic and disengaged and had only limited interest in public affairs. Second, because people were apathetic and disengaged, big business was able to buy influence in political parties. Business interests steered political parties away from important reforms and the result was that political officials controlled the government but did not represent the people who had voted them into office.

Dewey observed that Americans were now living in a new "Great Society" (Dewey 2008/1927, "The Public and its Problems," p. 314). In this new "machine age," advances in manufacturing, communication, and mass transportation had created a complex society replacing the democratic culture of small communities (Dewey 2008/1927, "The Public and its Problems," p. 314). And a new urban democratic culture, one that brought this sense of community to large metropolitan areas, had not yet emerged. The reasons for this were complex.

To begin with, Dewey noted that in the new machine age, Americans were faced with a number of economic uncertainties that affected their ability to own and operate farms and small businesses. It was difficult to anticipate when the demand for their goods might rise or fall. Often the costs of fertilizer, raw materials, and equipment were difficult to anticipate because their suppliers, cross-country corporations focused on maximizing their profit, operated in an unregulated free market. Similarly, unskilled workers were also subject to the ebbs and flows of a labor market that was unpredictable and organized to benefit large employers, not employees. And, of course, this was before the age of public unemployment insurance, employer subsidized health care, Medicare for the elderly, and social security for older people unable to continue working. The sheer complexity of these circumstances prevented people from accurately assessing the nature of their problems. Without understanding the causes of their problems, people were usually unable to understand and then act in ways that promoted their needs and interests. Furthermore, the needs and interests of the people varied considerably depending on where they lived in the country and how they were employed. Without a clear understanding of our problems, needs, and interests, Dewey stated, developing good solutions was nearly impossible. In words that seem as fitting today as they did a century ago, Dewey wrote that people "are caught in the sweep of forces too vast to understand or master. Thought is brought to a standstill and action paralyzed" (Dewey 2008/1927, "The Public and its Problems," p. 319). The best way forward, Dewey argued, was for people to come together, even in the most difficult and trying circumstances, identify their common needs and interests, and then act collectively. In other words, America needed more community and not more government. This theme was built on Dewey's earlier works. As he had stated in *Democracy and Education*, a democracy entailed much more than the institutions used to manage the state. A democracy must be embedded in "all modes of human association" and not just the political dimension of the society (Dewey 2008/1927, "The Public and its Problems," p. 325).

Dewey argued that the creation of a Great Community, a cultural democracy or as he sometimes said, a progressive democracy, would require the satisfaction of certain conditions. Satisfaction of these conditions would not guarantee the creation of the Great Community. But they were necessary conditions that would need to be satisfied before further progress was possible. The first of these was that people would need to recognize that their ability to understand human experience is dependent on their ability to communicate effectively with others. Dewey's own life experiences taught him that in a modern democracy, the members of the community have different needs and interests as a result of their age, gender, race, ethnicity, social class, religion, and employment. When poorly understood, these differences can easily lead to isolation and division. But, Dewey believed, when people reach out to one another, come out of their homes, and communicate openly about their needs and interests, diversity can become a strength, a source of new information that can help solve problems. Stated in other words, when people come together to discuss and then articulate their needs and interests, the potential for identifying shared needs increases substantially and the community gains a power that goes far beyond the individual right to vote.

Yes, Dewey acknowledged, the political machinery of a democracy is organized on the basis of individuals acting as individuals, going to the voting booth, and then electing representatives. But what was much more important was the articulation of shared interests by a community that could then drive reforms, not just on election day, but throughout the year. The greatest challenge to creating an awareness of shared needs and interests was that the public was becoming increasingly scattered and mobile and this prevented close interaction.

The second requirement for developing the Great Community was that the people, acting in concert with one another, would need to create the symbols and signs of their community to express and record progress toward greater democracy. Traditionally, the progress of democracy was marked by political elections and remembered on government holidays. But these elections and events comprised a narrative of democracy that was inescapably limited to the past; to a history that was rooted in government officials and political institutions. Dewey also asked his readers to recognize that in the Great Society, business and industry were providing the dominant symbols and signs that provided the narrative of the nation. In other words, progress was being recorded in the language of new products, new services, and new entertainment. This was a shallow way to understand the progress of humanity. Only when people acting in concert developed their own symbols and signs, or as we would say, a language, could the narrative of the nation be recovered and focused on the expansion of democracy.

A third precondition for the emergence of the Great Community was that members would need to have "freedom of social inquiry and of distribution of its conclusions" (Dewey 2008/1927, "The Public and its Problems," p. 339). And Dewey's notion of free social inquiry and freedom of expression went far beyond the traditional legalistic definition of these freedoms. Dewey observed that many people assumed they were free to address important issues simply because there was no legal prohibition. But, for him, this was absurd. As he had observed in his own career, free social inquiry was routinely compromised by intellectual habits that limited our ability to think clearly. One such limiting intellectual habit was, "a truly religious idealization of, and reverence for, established institutions; for example in our own politics, the Constitution, the Supreme Court, private property, free contract and so on" (Dewey 2008/1927, "The Public and its Problems," p. 341). In the United States, these revered institutions protected many important rights and freedoms. But, of course, they were not perfect. They protected some interests but not others. And in every case they were the consequence of custom and affirmed in political debates limited to a very small number of people. Of course, Dewey was not calling for the wholesale overthrow of these institutions. He was suggesting, however, that they be improved in order to protect a wider range of needs and interests. On the matter of change Dewey reminded his readers that

> There is a social pathology which works powerfully against effective inquiry into social institutions and conditions. It manifests itself in a thousand ways; in querulousness, in impotent drifting, in uneasy snatching at distractions, in—342—idealization of the long established, in a facile optimism assumed as a cloak, in riotous glorification of things "as they are," in intimidation of all dissenters (Dewey 2008/1927, "The Public and its Problems," pp. 341–2)

Inquiry into social institutions and practices was also limited by the belief that the material world, through the use of science, was capable of being understood and controlled while human society was not. This explained why many Americans viewed conditions such as child labor and poverty as beyond the control of human society. A Great Community that secured freedom of social inquiry and distribution of its conclusions would be much more capable in naming bad intellectual habits and disassembling the social pathologies that reinforced the status quo.

Fourth, Dewey argued that the development of the Great Community would require a more practical understanding and application of the social sciences in the development of public policy. His concern was that many social problems in the Great Society did not neatly map onto the theories and methodologies adopted within a particular discipline. For example, problems such as crime concerned issues were commonly addressed within several disciplines (e.g., sociology, political science, economics). The study of these problems, as examined at the university, was often beholden to theories that were outdated and artificially isolated by discipline. As I have noted, Dewey emphasized the importance of focusing on contemporary and local problems as a way to advance understanding of social conditions. Therefore he believed universities should prioritize teaching and research that focused on contemporary and local problems whether or not this aligned with the disciplines. This was a theme that pervaded much of his work and he often called for social inquiry that was "quotidian" and by this he meant, focused on the daily, real life events in the community.

A fifth requirement was that findings from research on social problems needed to reach as many people as possible. Dewey frowned upon dissemination that only reached a technical or "high-brow" audience (Dewey 2008/1927, "The Public and its Problems," p. 349). So, he saw academic journals as important but limited in facilitating social inquiry. Because Dewey viewed the arts as a valuable tool in framing and illuminating social problems, he argued for freedom of artistic expression, especially in literary presentations, which he saw as a particularly valuable device to critically examine social conditions.

In summary, Dewey's *The Public and Its Problems* accepted Lippmann's diagnosis of the limitations of early twentieth century American democracy. However, he rejected the journalist's call for an expansion of the government and the creation of a new federal bureaucracy. For Dewey, the arrival of the Great Society had brought many new conveniences and advancements that improved the quality of life for many Americans. But, a transformation to the Great Community would require a radical change in the American society. Dewey understood that such a transformation would require extraordinary commitment and effort. But, he saw development of the Great Community as the only plausible solution for a nation that had long outgrown the democracy associated with the small quiet mono-cultural towns of the past.

Conclusion

After World War I, Dewey's works concerning democracy began to examine the individual and social conditions that impeded the development of such a society. In *The Public and Its Problems*, he also began to articulate the essential conditions of a specific kind of modern democracy, a Great Community. He explained that in this democracy, social conflict is most effectively managed through an educational process that helps people focus on their social problems in collaboration with others. This process, best handled at schools and colleges committed to the community, could help people learn how to take the lead in identifying and solving their own problems.

Dewey noted that the development of the Great Community could be impeded by individual and social conditions. These included thoughtless habits that became dispositions, ignoring new discoveries about human society. The control of government and media by wealthy insiders also posed a serious challenge to the advancement of democracy. These individual and social conditions remained in place, however, because the public was becoming more isolated and distracted by life in the Great Society.

For Dewey, the only effective way for people to advance their democracy was to work toward the creation of a Great Community. And the necessary conditions for creating the Great Community were, (a) recognizing that an understanding of human experience depends on effective communication with others, (b) creating a narrative to express and record progress toward greater democracy, (c) securing free social inquiry and widely disseminating its conclusions, (d) focusing the social research capacity of the society on "quotidian" problems, and (e) disseminating research findings to as many people as possible. Realization of the Great Community would also need to reflect the values Dewey described in *Democracy and Education* and it would need to incorporate the deliberate educational systems he described in this earlier work. By the late 1920s Dewey was completing the positive description and explanation of what a cultural or progressive democracy would look like in the United States. Over the next 15 years he would continue to write about democracy and education. But, his focus became more specific as he addressed the economic and social conditions that created a growing gap between rich and poor, exacerbated and illuminated by the Great Depression.

10

Dewey and the Great Depression

Introduction

Dewey's publication of *The Public and its Problems* in 1927 added another substantial volume to his bookshelf and he soon received new invitations to speak from around the world. In the summer of 1928 he traveled to London, Paris, Berlin, Leningrad, and Moscow. In the summer of 1929 he visited London, Edinburgh, Frankfurt, and Vienna. Although these trips were not all business (his daughter Lucy was living in Vienna), he was the rare academic with a truly international reputation. During this period, Dewey received honorary degrees from the University of St Andrews, the University of Paris, and the University of Johannesburg. These international credentials complemented honorary degrees he received from American universities: Columbia, Harvard, and the University of California at Los Angeles.

As the Great Depression took hold in 1930, Dewey stepped up his writing and speaking on issues important to women, workers, and political dissenters. For instance, in January 1932, he wrote for *The Nation* advocating the repeal of laws prohibiting the distribution of information on birth control. In December 1932, he participated in a campaign to raise funds for the struggling Brookwood Labor College located in Katonah, New York. In 1933, Dewey advocated for the removal of legal restrictions barring Emma Goldman from visiting the United States. Throughout the Great Depression, Dewey took an intense interest in the plight of working families and repeatedly called upon President Hoover and then President Roosevelt to speed up relief efforts to benefit those who had lost their homes and jobs.

Dewey's increasing interest in public affairs was also reflected in his taking on new leadership responsibilities in progressive advocacy groups. He served as President of the People's Lobby and as Vice President of the League for Industrial Democracy (Ratner 2008). Perhaps the most important of these new posts came with his election as Chairman of the newly formed League for Independent Political Action (the LIPA) in September 1929. The LIPA was a national advocacy group established by progressives to advance reforms in social policy (Kurtz, Introduction to LW#5). The LIPA called for greater regulation of child labor in factories, increased legal protection of organized labor, and new government programs to provide Americans with unemployment insurance, pensions, and health care. Although the organization would fold before the end of the 1930s, it represented a new voice that helped articulate a progressive political agenda and Dewey was its leader.

Dewey produced six works during the 1930s that examined issues relevant to democracy, education, and the major social problems facing the nation (Dewey 1930/2008, "Individualism, Old and New"; "American Education Past and Future," 1931/2008; "Education for a Changing Social Order," 1934/2008; "The Need for Orientation," 1935/2008; "Liberalism and Social Action," 1935/2008; and "Freedom and Culture," 1939/2008). These publications were framed, at least in part, by the impact of the Great Depression, the emergence of totalitarianism in Europe, and the continuing industrialization and modernization of American society. They also presented some of Dewey's most pointed critiques of American society and its capitalist economy. His goal in these writings was not to revisit the relationship between education and democracy. Nor was it to say more about the Great Community. In these works, critique was the objective. He critiqued the dominant philosophical account of individualism and traditional liberalism. He critiqued the way American colleges prepared teachers for schools. And he critiqued the growing power of unregulated capitalism. In each case he remained optimistic about the prospects for positive social change. But he also sought to explain why the nation was unable to create a new progressive democracy.

Living and learning in a corporatized society

In 1930, Dewey completed a series of articles for the *New Republic* that were then published as *Individualism, Old and New* (Dewey 2008/1930, "Individualism, Old and New."). In this thin book, Dewey observed that individualism had always been an important part of American culture. But its meaning had changed radically over the preceding 100 years. In the early nineteenth century, the early pioneers settling the Midwest and the West believed in a variant of individualism that said Americans were free and equal, by nature. Of course, this belief was blind to the historical oppression of women and people of color. But it did provide pioneers with a sense of optimism. No matter what hardships were encountered, they believed they could always move on and make a new life for themselves on open land out west. In the early decades of the twentieth century, this belief in the land of opportunity was still held up as the exemplar of American individualism. But with the establishment of a new industrial economy dominated by large corporations, land was no longer the primary and widely distributed form of wealth. Instead, corporations dominated the economy and controlled the transportation, communications, and manufacturing industries. This resulted in the consolidation of great wealth in a small part of the population: large corporate shareholders.

Dewey noted that the industrial economy had also created a new generation of workers who toiled together in factories and lived next to one another in poor neighborhoods. But this new intimacy was only a matter of proximity. People who worked and lived in close proximity often had little to do with one another in a cultural or social sense and this limited their outlook on life. Life for most factory workers was simply a matter of surviving from day to day. Wealthy individuals lived entirely different lives and had little to do with the working class. Dewey argued that these stark divisions left many people bewildered and confused. Both rich and poor had become alienated or "lost individuals" because of their detachment from traditional communities and the social and cultural values that guided them (Dewey 2008/1930, "Individualism, Old and New," p. 66).

In the past, the school brought people together and prepared them for life in rural communities. And schools had now established vocational education programs to prepare children for work. But now they were failing to prepare students to think critically about the very difficult problems their society was facing—unemployment, poverty, and the inequitable distribution of wealth and income. Schools were not alone in this failing. Colleges and universities were also ineffective in preparing students for the challenges they would encounter in a corporatized society. Many college students had simply checked out and were amusing themselves with frivolous entertainment. As Dewey wrote,

> the distinguishing trait of the American student body in our higher schools is a kind of intellectual immaturity. This immaturity is mainly due to their enforced mental seclusion; there is, in their schooling, little free and disinterested concern with the underlying social problems of our civilization. (Dewey 2008/1930, "Individualism, Old and New," p. 102)

It was hardly surprising, therefore, that many Americans, even those well educated, were perplexed by the onset of the Great Depression. Soon, the traditional optimism and confidence of American individualism had been replaced by pessimism and despair. Workers worried about losing their jobs and the prospects of living on the street. Political elections were driven by fear. A new modern individualism had taken hold and was distinguished by feelings of isolation, insecurity, and fear.

Wealthy Americans viewed the unfolding social tragedies from their motorcars. Some generously supported the relief agencies that sprung up to help the new mass of homeless. But others, perceiving the crisis as inevitable or too difficult to tackle, declined to get involved. With the nation in an economic and social tailspin, many Americans, secure in their homes and jobs, simply watched as others lost everything. These spectator Americans were content to "glorify the past, . . . instead of seriously asking how we are to employ the means at our disposal so as to form an equitable and stable society" (Dewey 2008/1930, "Individualism, Old and New,"p. 48).

Dewey argued that recovery from these dire circumstances was possible. But it would require that people seriously acknowledge the great changes produced by the new industrial economy. Then, each would need to take responsibility for being a positive force for change. This change would begin, Dewey said, when people became more integrated with the world (Dewey 2008/1930, "Individualism, Old and New"). And this would require that each do his part to "cultivate his own garden" keeping in mind that our "garden" was a part of nature, closely connected to the world, and physically adjacent to our neighbors' homes (Dewey 2008/1930, "Individualism, Old and New," p. 122).

Educational barriers to achieving the Great Community

In February 1934, in Cleveland, Ohio, Dewey gave a speech at the national meeting of the American Association of Teachers Colleges. The speech was titled *Education for a Changing Social Order*, and it is usually overshadowed by Dewey's more popular works (Dewey 2008/1934, "Education for a Changing Social Order"). But here Dewey examined one of the great limitations to progressive change in American society, that is, the American school's subject-centered curriculum. The subject-centered curriculum was plagued by two serious limitations. First, it ignored any meaningful instruction about the society's great contemporary problems. Second, it was taught with a method that asked students to find the correct answer to a conceptual or abstract problem. Dewey called upon teacher colleges and teachers to take the lead in addressing both of these limitations.

Students who completed school without any significant understanding of the society's great contemporary problems were often left with the impression that the status quo was simply the way life was lived. Good citizens had a duty to endure tough times, but not to change them. Also, students taught through a "find the correct answer approach" were seldom prompted to examine the problem's underlying causes. Both of these limitations produced a passive population unprepared to think critically about their democracy. And the creation of a passive population was especially problematic when viewed in the context of the nation's serious social, economic, and political problems.

Dewey observed that the new industrial economy provided wealthy businessmen with new financial power to influence the political system. But it also gave them the communication and transportation technologies that let them exercise this power with more speed and precision across the nation. And yet many Americans simply accepted this new level of class-based power and influence as inevitable, as a given. This passive posture had serious negative consequences. As Dewey noted, in the industrial era, "economic forces decide political activity" and "operate in ways that are not open and clear to the mass of the citizens" (Dewey 2008/1934, "Education for a Changing Social Order," p. 159). Therefore, although the need for a more critical perspective was clearly evident, schools were failing to help students understand the complexity of their society or the problems that left them lost and confused.

Dewey argued that teacher colleges had an important responsibility to prepare teachers who could help students think critically. But helping students become more critical thinkers entailed more than just a change in teaching practice. It would also require changes in the school subject-centered curriculum. A new school curriculum would need to reflect the reality that life in a democratic modern society is constantly changing and posing new problems that need to be solved.

Here, Dewey was gently reminding his audience of what had always been true about American education. The standard subject-centered curriculum required that students learn a great deal of information that they will never use as adults. This curriculum was stable and easy for teachers to master. It was easy for schools to administer. But it left students unprepared for life. A new curriculum that taught mathematics, science, and history in relevant and meaningful ways would need to be developed and implemented. And, he argued, it would need to be taught through a critical problem-solving approach that transcended the *entire* school and all subjects.

Dewey's remarks to the American Association of Teachers Colleges were not his only words during the 1930s on how American education needed to be reformed. In June 1935, *Forum* magazine published an exchange between Dewey and Tyler Dennett, a historian who was, at the time, president of Williams College. The brief exchange highlighted Dewey's increasing concern that American educational institutions were not preparing students to think critically about political and social problems. Dennett acknowledged that schools and colleges needed to improve. But, he argued, they were improving incrementally and any school or college was inevitably bound to (or limited by) the democratically elected leaders given governing responsibility for the institution.

Dewey's exchange with Dennett is important for us because in Dewey's piece, *The Need for Orientation*, he offered a justification for innovation at schools and colleges along with a dire statement of the negative consequences if educators continued to accept the status quo (Dewey 2008/1935, *The Need for Orientation*). Dewey began with the qualification that his critique was not focused on teachers and professors but on a culture that exhibited almost no interest in preparing young people for a world that would be significantly different in the future. For Dewey, too many American schools and colleges relied on the mechanical "find the correct answer" approach that precluded any opportunity to develop critical thinking skills.

Dewey's readers understood that in the United States, education was primarily a local and state responsibility and this precluded development of national educational priorities. But the complex problems facing the country transcended local and state boundaries. And local and state education authorities often represented the status quo and had little interest in substantial change. Consequently, curricula remained stagnant. Stagnant courses left "young people . . . with no clue to the situation in which they are to live and . . . at a loss intellectually and morally, as well as vocationally" (Dewey 2008/1935, *The Need for Orientation*, p. 164) Students who left schools and colleges unable to understand their society were especially vulnerable to the forces of propaganda, forces which at the time were contributing to the rise of Fascism in Germany and Italy.

For Dewey, the lack of any bona fide commitment to improving students' critical thinking skills almost ensured the production of a generation with limited capacity to lead change. This kind of educational culture, in turn, reflected the drift in American society, a nation in 1935 that was struggling to address its critical economic, social, and political problems. In this sense, sadly, schools and colleges mirrored the society. But they were not an innocuous mirror. As Dewey stated, "the mirror is not passive. It serves to perpetuate the social and economic conditions" by teaching students to accept the status quo while steering them away from new perspectives that might lead to change (Dewey 2008/1935, *The Need for Orientation*, p. 165).

Dewey had repeatedly criticized educational institutions for teaching a subject-centered curriculum that failed to prepare students for a more complex future. This was a point he developed earlier in *Education for a Changing Social Order*. But now his critique extended to noting that schools and colleges also play a powerful role in affirmatively securing privilege and inequality. Educators, he argued, have a responsibility to recognize this and then transform their institutions into the wellsprings of innovation needed to help create the Great Community.

Cultural barriers to achieving the Great Community

In 1935, the United States was struggling to escape the effects of the Great Depression. Although the nation's highest unemployment numbers of 1933 were in the past, nobody knew where the country was headed. President Franklin Roosevelt, elected in November 1932, had campaigned for reelection arguing that Americans needed a new deal. The New Deal programs would eventually include (a) a major federal relief effort to employ workers through the construction of new public buildings, roads, and other projects; (b) the establishment of the social security pension for the elderly; and (c) federal legislation recognizing the right to collective bargaining. These programs, first rejected by the political system but finally accepted, helped sustain millions of Americans as the nation crept out of the Great Depression (Kennedy 1999). The challenges posed by the Great Depression were soon overshadowed, however, by the rise of Fascism under Adolf Hitler in Germany and the growth of Communism under Joseph Stalin in the Soviet Union.

Hitler came to power in January 1933 through democratic elections and soon consolidated his power by shutting down political opponents and establishing a secret police agency (the Gestapo). The Nazi regime enacted laws instituting a policy of anti-Semitism that eventually led to the Holocaust and the murder of 6 million Jews. Millions of other Europeans regarded by the Nazi state as genetically inferior (racial minorities, gays and lesbians, and persons with disabilities) were exiled, imprisoned, or killed. Hitler also used his dictatorial powers to stimulate the German economy, especially through large government purchases of military hardware. By 1936 the nation had made what appeared to be a stunning economic recovery with almost full employment (Paxton and Hessler 2011).

Joseph Stalin rose to national power in the Soviet Union in the early 1920s. When Vladimir Lenin died in 1924, Stalin consolidated his control of the Communist Party bureaucracy. During the 1920s and 1930s, Stalin transformed the mostly agrarian Soviet economy to one dominated by large-scale manufacturing and collective farming. Both the factories and farms were state owned. Stalin also established prison labor camps where hundreds of thousands of dissenters and political opponents were imprisoned. These extreme and inhumane measures had the desired effect, however. Productivity rose and the Soviet economy lurched forward while most of the world was still struggling.

Dewey's work in *Liberalism and Social Action* and *Freedom and Culture* responded to the belief held by many Americans that the greatest threats to freedom came from tyrannical governments and not from other institutions or forces in the society. Dewey was well aware of the dangers posed to humanity by the leaders of Nazi Germany and the Communist Soviet Union. He understood that the American government had occasionally lapsed in its defense of freedom and persecuted its own citizens. Indeed, Dewey's work in the early civil rights movement, his support for immigrants, and his sympathies with organized labor made him a person of interest in several investigations conducted by the Federal Bureau of Investigation. In other words, Dewey understood that governments could commit the most egregious crimes. But he also saw how a blind faith in economic forces, operating in "the free market," also posed serious impediments to achieving the Great Community.

In *Liberalism and Social Action*, Dewey provided a history and critique of traditional eighteenth-century liberalism, an outdated political philosophy that effectively obscured dangers posed by unregulated economic forces. This book was based on a series of lectures given at the University of Virginia in April 1935 and in it Dewey argued that the traditional liberalism of the eighteenth century was right to argue for the existence of certain natural rights. After all, this was an era in which the British monarchy had governed its American colonies arbitrarily and capriciously. But the traditional liberalism, which provided a compelling response to the *government* abuses in the eighteenth century, now offered little to mitigate the harm Americans were suffering at the hands of an unregulated *capitalist economy.* Freedom in the early twentieth century required more than a democratically elected government. It required protection from the economic forces that arbitrarily and capriciously left millions of Americans destitute and unable to support themselves. As Dewey explained, three significant changes had occurred since the founding of the American republic and these revealed the poor fit between traditional liberalism and life in a modern society.

First, in the eighteenth and nineteenth centuries, many communities were plagued by a genuine scarcity of food, shelter, and clothing. Pilgrims and pioneers often died as a result of starvation or exposure to the elements. By the early twentieth century, however, developments in agriculture, transportation, and communication gave the nation the capacity to produce an ample supply of food, clothing, and shelter. Still, during the Great Depression, many Americans only avoided starvation through breadlines and begging in the streets. These circumstances confirmed, Dewey explained, that the nation had effectively chosen to continue an economic system based on unlimited property rights and an unregulated free market, even when these institutions abandoned millions to poverty (Dewey 2008/1935, "Liberalism and Social Action," p. 43).

Second, Dewey observed, a scarcity of basic goods (e.g., food, clothing) was a genuine feature of early American society. And this scarcity pushed people to acquire the financial resources to purchase and store the supplies needed to sustain them during periods of hardship. This fear of scarcity had positive consequences for a nation that needed to build new roads, canals, businesses, and cities. It provided the motivation to save the capital needed to finance important and socially useful building and construction projects. Of course, Dewey noted, the scarcity of basic goods (e.g., food and clothing), which had been genuine in the eighteenth century, was no longer real. And the unrestricted accumulation of capital no longer had the same positive consequences for the nation. Wealthy capitalists now had the ability and the right to acquire as much wealth as they desired. They could manage this wealth as they wished, even when this led to the loss of employment for workers with no other means to support themselves. Again, Dewey noted, the times had changed and the values of traditional liberalism did not align with the more urgent needs of the society.

Third, Dewey noted that in the days of the early Republic, farmers, merchants, and craftsmen believed that the nation's growth was best assured if each adult male was free to act independently to satisfy his individual needs and ambitions. Accordingly, there was no great interest in coordinating the work and investment of peoples' labor unless this maximized individual success. During the 1930s this mindset was still prevalent. But, Dewey contended, the historical justification for unfettered individual ambition was now outdated. The nation's progress was not best advanced by the uncoordinated efforts of selfish individuals. Progress, for the society as a whole, was best assured through the kind of cooperation and collaboration evidenced in New Deal programs. Perhaps more importantly, eighteenth-century liberalism, which valorized private property and free markets, failed to recognize the social realities of a new industrialized society where large cities needed more coordinated means to address problems such as poverty and unemployment.

Given these changes, and the poor fit between traditional American liberalism and the new industrial economy, Dewey called for a new American liberalism. The normative force of a new liberalism would not focus on private property or free markets. Instead, it would emphasize the moral importance of personal growth and the development of democratic communities. To be sure, Dewey's arguments against eighteenth century liberalism were based, at least in part, on generalizations that his critics challenged. Not every community had been dominated by a philosophy that emphasized scarcity, financial security, and individual success. But his central criticism held. The new industrialized economy of the 1930s rewarded those who acted in accordance with traditional liberalism. It had little sympathy for those who paused to help others and, in the process, risked their own well-being. A new form of liberalism was needed and in *Liberalism and Social Action*, Dewey worked hard to show how traditional liberalism failed to align with the needs of a population living and working in a modern society.

In 1939, at the age of 80, Dewey published *Freedom and Culture*, a work that took on the task of explaining the relationship between culture and freedom in contemporary America. Dewey began by noting that in a modern industrialized society, people were exposed to "impersonal forces" that were "undreamed of in the early days of the Republic" (Dewey 2008/1939, "Freedom and Culture," p. 104). These impersonal forces worked "on a vast scale, with causes and effects so remote as not to be perceptible" (Dewey 2008/1939, "Freedom and Culture," p. 104). Thus, Dewey observed, in the 1930s, especially during the worst years of the Great Depression, life was contingent. The failure of a bank would often deprive a worker of his life's savings and this, in turn, would lead to the loss of the family home. When tragedies like this struck, many Americans struggled to understand what was happening to them. They had not anticipated that their freedom could be limited in this manner. Instead, many Americans viewed their government (or foreign governments) as posing the greatest threat to their freedom. But, Dewey noted, social, economic, legal, and technological conditions (broadly understood as "culture") were a powerful force that could easily match or exceed the coercive power of any government.

Dewey explained that Americans failed to understand the influence of culture on their freedom, at least in part, because they had been brought up to believe that no other force could arbitrarily jeopardize life and liberty like the government. And, in the eighteenth century, for most Americans, this view made sense. But as the industrial economy transformed the nation, it became clear that new corporations were gaining immense powers of a kind never seen before. Many of these powers were grounded in the institution of private property. If a corporation owned a railroad or a factory, its use of these assets, even when resulting in harm to the community, was regarded as legitimate. Because Americans viewed their political freedoms as intact, the hardships they endured at the hands of corporations were accepted as unfortunate but legal and moral. Business leaders and politicians would remind the public that such hardships were the consequence of legitimate property rights, legal rights ostensibly enjoyed by all Americans. But, Dewey observed, Americans who believed this folly were surrendering their future to impersonal and unforgiving forces in the culture that were as dangerous as any government. They had failed to recognize that their culture, now dominated by economic interests, was undermining and, indeed, eroding the democracy that had gradually developed in communities across the country.

Democracy could only be protected and advanced, Dewey argued, if it was a priority across the culture and not just in the political sphere. He wrote, "The struggle for democracy has to be maintained on as many fronts as culture has aspects: political, economic, international, educational, scientific and artistic, religious" (Dewey 2008/1939, "Freedom and Culture," p. 186). A commitment to individual growth and democratic communities as a part of human association needed to be the highest priority in all aspects of the culture. Simply relying on political institutions to solve the great problems was no longer a feasible strategy to advance American democracy.

And how could freedom and democracy be advanced across the culture? Dewey returned to his long-held belief that such progress needed to be made in "face to face associations" in communities committed to the kind of communications where "emotions and ideas are shared as well as joint undertakings engaged in" (Dewey 2008/1939, "Freedom and Culture," p. 176). Or, to make the point in a slightly differently way, Dewey repeated the words he had written 12 years earlier in *The Public and its Problems*, "Democracy must begin at home, and its home is the neighborly community" (Dewey 2008/1939, "Freedom and Culture," p. 176).

Conclusion

In the 1930s, Dewey's writing focused on a series of problems that undermined the development of the American democracy. These included an outdated sense of individualism; the isolation, insecurity and fear that many encountered in living in a corporatized society; the inability of schools and colleges to prepare students for tackling the great problems of the society; and the tendency many Americans had to overlook the adverse consequences generated by an unregulated free market economy. Dewey's works were certainly informed by his observations of the hardships Americans endured as they struggled to survive during the Great Depression. But they were also fueled by the awareness that these hardships were exacerbated by a culture that secured the privilege of the wealthy. Unfortunately, the nation's schools and colleges reinforced the status quo and failed to teach students how to think critically. They operated, as Dewey observed, as temporal mirrors ensuring that the future would look much like the past. Dewey never lost his optimism about the future of the American democracy. But in the 1930s he provided a clear punch list of the many cultural beliefs and institutions that would need to be reformed in order to achieve a better democracy. And the list was long.

11

The Deweyan community college

Introduction

The central premise of this essay is that the American community college has reached a crossroads. Since the 1947 Truman Commission Report, community colleges have been focused on expanding educational opportunity. With the onset of the Financial Crisis and the Great Recession, however, a new priority has emerged—college completion. Completion Agenda advocates argue that colleges and universities need to improve their college completion rates for two reasons. First, they say, higher completion rates will improve the nation's economic growth. Second, higher completion rates will help arrest the nation's increasing income inequality. There is evidence to support both claims. However, no one can guarantee that improved completion rates will solve either economic problem. The solution to these economic problems, in other words, may not lie in the realm of education. Furthermore, community colleges have been asked to improve their completion rates at a time when institutions are operating in an environment that is becoming increasingly uncertain. Each of the five major drivers (income inequality, technological change and learning analytics, globalization, generational equity issues, and public higher education funding) could significantly alter the needs of students enrolling at the institution. These drivers could significantly change the way colleges operate and deliver the programs and services. Lastly, the five drivers are likely to radically restructure the way many governments, corporations, and other organizations carry out their work. The significance of these drivers is that the relatively stable environment within which colleges now operate—framed by government funding, a steady labor market, and the desire for traditional curricula—cannot be predicted for the future. Community colleges will need to make strategic decisions – in response to these drivers – more quickly and more effectively if they are to remain leaders in delivering open access postsecondary education. It is within this uncertain environment, therefore, that community colleges have now been asked to prioritize completion and, in the process, address national economic problems.

As I showed earlier, community colleges have been called upon to address state and national problems in the past. During the 1960s and 1970s, community colleges in California were instrumental in expanding educational access while limiting enrollment pressures on the state's public universities. Community college faculty and staff employed a cooling out process that quietly redirected students unprepared for university study. Community colleges were also key in expanding educational opportunity after the passage of the GI Bill, the 1964 Civil Rights Act, and the Higher Education Act of 1965. During World War II, junior colleges played an important role in training military personnel and workers to be employed in war industries. During the Great Depression, junior colleges played an active role in facilitating federal financial aid programs. The federal government also used the junior college concept to establish emergency junior colleges to employ laid-off teachers and educate unemployed students. During the first decades of the twentieth century, the first junior colleges were established to strengthen high schools and universities and facilitate the transfer of students from one to another. These early junior college programs were also established to extend parental control over young students, to ensure church oversight of the college curriculum, to strengthen normal schools, to limit enrollment pressure at the university, and to provide private liberal arts colleges with the opportunity to reorganize and deliver a more focused and less expensive curriculum.

Of course, junior college and community college students were able to take advantage of opportunities offered by these institutions. No doubt many went on to university study and good careers—opportunities that would never have existed if these institutions were not in place. It is still true, however, that even today, after community colleges have evolved into fine institutions, the majority of students attending a community college do not graduate with the credential they desired when they enrolled. This was not a serious concern when the institution's top priority was accommodating other institutions or providing access. When we go back into the community college literature, it is difficult to find a substantial and sustained discussion about graduation rates. This simply was not a serious concern for the institutional outsiders who played a leading role in shaping community college education. Of course, today, after having suffered through the Financial Crisis and Great Recession, college completion is a big priority for institutional outsiders, and for good reason too. Every year, the federal and state governments make a huge investment in community colleges and their students. In this new era of austerity where government debt and student debt have increased to astronomical heights, institutional outsiders and students want more for their money. And who can blame them?

Still, it is difficult to find anyone in higher education opposed to higher completion rates. It is difficult to find anyone at the community college favoring a retreat on the traditional commitment to access. Community colleges *should* remain committed to access and they *should* achieve higher completion rates. But, I contend, this is a good time to consider accepting a higher duty— one that runs to the nation and its people and not to the government and institutional outsiders.

Community colleges are ideally organized and situated to attend to the personal educational needs of their students. They are well positioned to take an active role in contributing to the development of democratic communities. Indeed, many community colleges are doing this right now. The Democracy Commitment is just one example of an organic movement promoting civic engagement at community colleges (Kisker and Ronan 2012). Still, what most community colleges lack is a normative vision that organizes and validates commitments to individual growth and the development of democratic communities. When such commitments are only the result of servant leaders or an excellent faculty, they are not fully inscribed in the culture and history of the institution. A change in leadership or a transition in faculty can leave an institution on its heels, without its heart, and fixated on the budget.

In the preceding chapters, I have provided an admittedly brief review of an American philosopher and educator who consistently argued that education should be about something more than preparation for a job or university study. It should be about helping students grow and advancing our democracy. Dewey's arguments were well received in his day. He was granted many honors and after his death was described as the "conscience of the American people" (Commager 1950, p. 100). Sixty years later, it is hard to find many John Deweys in higher education. Those of us employed at colleges and universities work in an industry driven, now more than ever, by institutional rankings, enrollment reports, external funding, publish or perish, retention, completion, self support and entrepreneurial programs, and collegiate athletics. At most institutions, there is little time and even less funding to focus on student growth and the advancement of democracy. But, Dewey the optimist would say progress on recovering the appropriate aims for education is possible.

The priorities and values grounding Deweyan normative vision

Given the works reviewed earlier I suggest that the following eleven priorities and values would ground a Deweyan normative vision for community colleges. These points would need to be clarified to fit a particular institution but this kind of work is involved in any application of a normative vision. The first seven points concern the relationship that the community college, acting through its faculty and staff, should have with students. The next three describe priorities and values that help support creation of a democratic community on campus. The last point explains the relevancy of Dewey's observations on the relationship a community college has with the community, the state, and the society.

Priorities and values grounding instruction

First, as I have mentioned before, the development of a Deweyan normative vision would need to be guided by the realization that a central purpose of education is to promote individual growth. Colleges need to deliver curricula and courses in specific contexts. We should anticipate that much of traditional college operations would remain the same. Faculty must ensure that students progressing have the skills and knowledge required to complete their program. Staff need to manage the institution and non instructional services effectively and efficiently. However, Dewey would remind us that in working with students, our responsibility goes beyond delivering content, evaluating performance, and regulating the college experience. Seasoned faculty and staff know that student growth requires many different forms of support including attention, flexibility, rigor, direction, patience, compassion, formative assessment, and summative evaluation. The point here is that our interactions with students should always involve more than merely preparing them for transfer or employment. A commitment to education requires that we also provide students with a wide range of supports so they can have the experiences needed to become fully contributing members of a democratic community.

Second, a Deweyan normative vision would hold that students must leave the institution with an ability to interact constructively and freely with diverse communities in order to understand one another and build shared interests (Dewey 2008/1916, "Democracy and Education"). These interests cannot be prescribed by educators. But students must understand that life in a democratic community carries a responsibility to learn about others and support them when possible. Community life also gives us license to ask for help from others when needed.

Third, a community college education should ensure that all students acquire good intelligent thinking habits, habits that enable them to systematically analyze problems in collaboration with others (Dewey 2008/1922, "Human Nature and Conduct"). For Dewey, a student's development of a capacity for intelligent thinking or a reflective disposition was an essential responsibility for every educator. When students acquire this capacity they analyze problems carefully, systematically, and courageously. A reflective disposition is also the best assurance of avoiding prejudice and bias.

Fourth, a Deweyan would tell us that instruction needs to be presented with a "social perspective," that is, one that helps students understand their responsibility to be "useful to others through their work" no matter what field or career path they intend to follow (Dewey 2008/1913, "Education from a Social Perspective," MW#7, p. 126). Employment or university study should not be pursued simply to secure a comfortable life in the suburbs. Community college students, like their counterparts in professional schools, should be helped to develop an identity that carries responsibilities to their occupation and community.

Fifth, as Dewey wrote in *Democracy and Education*, preparing students for an occupation must include helping them understand the occupation's history, social relevancy, and place in the economy (Dewey 2008/1916, "Democracy and Education"). This kind of education can help students anticipate, understand, and manage significant changes in their employment. Helping students learn how to adapt after graduating was a high priority for Dewey. It should be just as important for us in preparing our students for their future.

Sixth, learning should be organized around shared problem solving (Dewey 2008/1916, "Democracy and Education."). A Deweyan normative vision would assert that this kind of activity helps students better understand their experiences. It also invites them to better understand the lives of their classmates. Instruction based on a model of shared problem solving helps develop the vital communication and interpersonal skills needed to sustain a healthy democratic community and successfully address problems as they arise. Finally, a discipline focused curriculum should be used when this advances student growth and not simply because it aligns with how faculty were trained in the past.

Seventh, community colleges must eliminate the institutional and personal incentives that lead faculty and staff to track students into one program or another. New reconstructed Deweyan curricula would be a synthesis of vocational and academic curricula, programs that would prepare students for an "occupation." (Dewey 2008/1916, "Democracy and Education"). Dewey was strongly opposed to the practice of tracking, a practice that, unfortunately, may be as prevalent today at some colleges as it was 100 years ago. This kind of tracking crushes student ambition, creates resentments that undermine the community, and often replicates class divisions.

Priorities and values guiding development of a democratic campus community

Dewey's writing on the Great Community in *The Public and its Problems* offers three insights into developing a democratic campus community (Dewey 2008/1927, "The Public and its Problems"). The first is based on his faith in the power of communication. Dewey was well aware of the different interests and needs that people have while living in a community. These different needs and interests are a consequence of our age, gender, race, ethnicity, religion, social class, and employment. Institutions that foreclose the opportunity to understand our differences often experience division. But when our different needs and interests are discussed, this brings a new potential to develop shared interests, solve problems, and move the college forward. Of course, at almost any community college, institutional challenges can be successfully addressed through effective leadership, wise planning, and prudent resource allocation. But Dewey recognized that in any institution, the power of traditional administrative directives often pales when compared to the power of a unified community committed to solving a problem without prompting or direction. The point here is that this power is only developed as a result of open communication where members of the community can first discuss their respective needs and then work to develop shared interests.

Second, community college education has become an industry with its own institutionalized language. Almost any community college employee would affirm that terms such as FTE, retention, and developmental studies carry a meaning that far exceeds what outsiders might imagine. These terms do not just identify unique parts of the business, however. They also select certain aspects of the institution's organizational life for special attention. Dewey recognized that in any institution, the language of the institution orders thought, opens up some options, and forecloses others. With this in mind, it is easy to see why the creation of a democratic campus community would be advanced by the creation of a language (the symbols and signs) that would identify the priorities and values of the community. We can now see why terms such as communication, shared interests, a reflective disposition, occupations, and quotidian research, have special meaning in a community of Deweyans. However, every college community would have a variety of interests, needs, and responsibilities that might be more clearly identified when addressed in a language that reflects and honors the best of its own culture.

Third, a normative vision guided by Dewey's work would state that the creation of a democratic campus community requires open or transparent inquiry into real problems experienced by the college's students, faculty, staff, and administrators. When findings are made, they should be widely disseminated in the organization. Dewey recognized that researchers tend to preference the data, methods, and theories with which they are most familiar. But these may not provide the best means of understanding a given problem. Consequently, he advocated for an approach to inquiry that was practical, relevant to the stakeholders, and transparent, whether or not this aligned with the interests of outsiders. Finally, on the matter of inquiry, a Deweyan normative vision would recognize that in any society there are those who will work hard to foreclose inquiry into policies, procedures, and the status quo. The creation of a democratic community on campus would be mindful of this pathology and use care to avoid repeating past practice simply because "that's how we have always done it."

Priorities and values guiding the institution's relationship with the community

A Deweyan normative vision would also have implications for how a community college interacts with communities in its service area. During the 1930s, and the dark days of the Great Depression, Dewey published several works that are relevant here. He criticized the American society for its great inequality in income and wealth. He criticized American schools and colleges for failing to inform students about the great social problems facing the country. And he criticized American culture for accepting an eighteenth-century narrative about the relationship between people and their society.

In each of these critiques, Dewey was responding to what he saw and experienced in his daily life. The Great Depression had left millions without a job while many wealthy Americans ignored the crisis and explained it as inevitable or insolvable. Because many schools and colleges ignored the serious social problems of the day, they inadvertently validated the status quo. And, as Dewey observed, many unemployed laborers accepted their plight because of their belief that governments (and not capitalists) posed the greatest threat to their freedom.

A community college guided by a Deweyan normative vision would have a responsibility to address serious problems harming the community, especially when well-educated faculty and staff were aware of them. Precisely how and when this might be done would be a matter for the college community. But, as Dewey pointed out, educational institutions have a duty to educate and through these means confront the injustices that the college community observes. The struggle for a better democracy is not something that can be left for the voting booth (Dewey 2008/1939, "Freedom and Culture").

Conclusion

It may be helpful at this point to remember why Dewey is a good figure to bring into a conversation about the future of community college education. These institutions now operate at a time when their traditional mission of access is being discounted and credential completion is being touted as the new priority. Of course, community college students want their institution to take both objectives seriously. But this debate reveals a problem that has long overshadowed the development of junior colleges and community colleges. Because community colleges lack the financial independence, high status, and rich history enjoyed by other colleges and universities, as a group of institutions, their role in the American system of education has been largely determined by outsiders. For most of the twentieth century, this mission was expanding educational opportunity. And the mission became the institution's normative vision. That is, expanding educational opportunity was not simply what these institutions were required to do; it was what all agreed they *should* do. Now, community colleges are being assigned another top priority, a worthy and fair assignment, but "assigned" nevertheless.

It is time community colleges, and the people who make them work, take a leadership role in determining their purposes, and specifically their moral responsibility to their students and the communities they serve. And, given the economic, political, and social environment that they and their students inhabit, I have argued that Dewey can provide guidance on this.

Of course, Dewey offers little help in carrying out the mechanics of community college education. His views are only helpful once we see that education is intimately connected to democracy and for all its blessings, the American democracy has room for improvement. What Dewey does offer, however, is a set of beliefs, a coherent philosophy, and a collection of priorities and values for a group of educators disappointed with a set of aspirations that goes no farther than access and completion. In considering the moral purposes of community college education, surely we can do better than access and completion.

Precisely how Dewey might be used, of course, is a matter to be left to individual colleges. Clearly, colleges would need to make inferences based on the priorities and values highlighted in this work. And some may use a little

Dewey, some may use a lot. Every college would be different. What Deweyan priorities and values offer, however, is a counterweight to the economy-driven vision being pushed by institutional outsiders and a polestar to guide them into the future. Most importantly, for the millions of students studying at community colleges today, a Deweyan normative vision provides them with the moral authority to step forward and legitimately claim a larger role in shaping the institution that may yet be "Democracy's College".

Bibliography

Abrams, R. M. (1989). "The U. S. Military and Higher Education: A Brief History." *Annals of the American Academy of Political and Social Science* 502: 15–28.

Addams, J. (2002). "The Subjective Necessity for Social Settlements," in J. B. Elshtain (ed.), *The Jane Addams Reader*. New York: Basic Books, pp. 14–28. (originally published in 1893).

Allen, J. S. and Allen, G. C. (1937). "The Need for Public Junior Colleges in New York State." *The School Review* 45(1): 38–52.

American Association of Community Colleges. (1988). *Building Communities: A Vision for a New Century*. Washington, D.C.: American Association of Community Colleges.

—(2012). *Reclaiming the American Dream: Community Colleges and the Nation's Future*. Washington, D.C.: American Association of Community Colleges.

—(2014). Community College Fact Sheet. Retrieved, April 10, 2014 from: http://www.aacc.nche.edu/AboutCC/Documents/Facts14_Data_R2.pdf

Anderson, T. H. (1995). *The Movement and the Sixties: Protest in America from Greensboro to Wounded Knee*. New York: Oxford University Press.

Archibald, R. B. (2002). *Redesigning the Financial Aid System: Why Colleges and Universities should Switch Roles with the Federal Government*. Baltimore, MD: Johns Hopkins University Press.

Aud, S., Hussar, W., Johnson, F., Kena, G., Roth, E., Manning, E., Wang, X. and Zhang, J. (2012). *The Condition of Education 2012*. Washington, D.C.: National Center for Education Statistics.

Barnes, L. and Hall, P. A. (2013). "Neoliberalism and social resilience in the developed democracies," in P. A. Hall and M. Lamont (eds), *Social Resilience in the Neoliberal Era*. New York: Cambridge University Press, pp. 209–38.

Baum, S. and Ma, J. (2011). *Trends in College Pricing, 2011*. Washington, DC: The College Board.

Baum, S., Ma, J. and Payea, K. (2013). *Education Pays, 2013*. Washington, DC: The College Board.

Baum, S. and Payea, K. (2011). *Trends in Student Aid, 2011*. Washington, DC: The College Board.

Baum, S., Payea, K. and Steele, P. (2009). *Trends in Student Aid, 2009*. Washington, D.C.: The College Board.

Berolzheimer, B. (1942). "Defense Activities at Woodrow Wilson." *Junior College Journal* 13(1): 13–16.

Bethel, L. L. and Wilson, J. W. (1942). "The Opportunity of Crises." *The Journal of Higher Education* 13(7): 370–3.

Birnbaum, R. (1988). *How Colleges Work: The Cybernetics of Academic Organization and Leadership*. San Francisco: Jossey-Bass.

Bishop, P. C. (2012). "The three horizons of educational change." *On the Horizon* 20(2): 137–44.

Bivens, J. (February 6, 2013). "Government Layoffs Are a Major Cause of Persistent Unemployment - Room for Debate," *The New York Times*, Retrieved June 13, 2013, from http://www.nytimes.com/roomfordebate/2013/02/06/are-government-layoffs-the-problem/government-layoffs-are-a-major-cause-of-persistent-unemployment

Blinder, A. S. (2013). *After the Music Stopped: The Financial Crisis, the Response, and the Work Ahead*. New York: Penguin Press.

Boydston, J. A. and Poulos, K. (1978). *Checklist of Writings about John Dewey*, 2d edn, 1887–1977. Carbondale, IL: Southern Illinois University Press.

Bracewell, R. H. (1935). "The Service of the Public Junior College in the Current Crisis." *The School Review* 43(7): 514–22.

Bragg, D. D. and Durham, B. (2012). "Perspectives on Access and Equity in the Era of (Community) College Completion." *Community College Review* 40(2): 106–25.

Branson, H. (1942). "The Role of the Negro College in the Preparation of Technical Personnel for the War Effort." *The Journal of Negro Education* 11(3): 297–303.

Briggs, X. de S. (2008). *Democracy as Problem Solving: Civic Capacity in Communities across the Globe*. Cambridge, MA: The MIT Press.

Brint, S. and Karabel, J. (1989). *The Diverted Dream: Community Colleges and the Promise of Educational Opportunity in America, 1900–1985*. New York: Oxford University Press.

Brothers, E. Q. (1930). "Legal Status of the Publicly Supported Junior College. June, 1929." *The School Review* 38(10): 737–49.

Brown, J. S. (1901). "The Joliet Township High School." *The School Review* 9(7): 417–32.

Brown, M. B. (2009). *Science in Democracy: Expertise, Institutions, and Representation*. Cambridge, MA: The MIT Press.

Brose, E. D. (2010). *A History of the Great War: World War One and the International Crisis of the early Twentieth Century*. New York: Oxford University Press.

Brynjolfsson, E. and McAfee, A. (2012). *Race against the Machine: How the Digital Revolution is Accelerating Innovation, Driving Productivity, and Irreversibly Transforming Employment and the Economy*. Lexington, MA: Digital Frontier Press.

Buddy, F. (1990). *George Frederick Zook: An Analysis of Selected Contributions of an American Educator*. Akron, OH: University of Akron.

Bureau of the Census (1942). *Sixteenth Census of the United States: 1940*. Washington, D.C.: Department of Commerce.

Burrell, B. J. and Eckelberry, R. H. (1934). "The Free Public High School in the Post-Civil-War Period. I. Political, Social, Moral, and Religious Arguments." *The School Review* 42(8): 606–14.

Callan, P. M. (2009). *California Higher Education, the Master Plan, and the Erosion of College Opportunity*. Washington, D.C.: The National Center for Public Policy and Higher Education.

Cardozier, V. R. (1993). *Colleges and Universities in World War II*. Westport, CT: Praeger.

Carnevale, A. P. and Rose, S. J. (2011). *The Undereducated American.* Washington DC: The Center on Education and the Workforce, Georgetown University.

Cervero, R. M. and Wilson, A. L. (1994). *Planning Responsibly for Adult Education: A Guide to Negotiating Power and Interests,* 1st edn. San Francisco: Jossey-Bass Publishers.

Clark, B. R. (1960a). "The 'Cooling Out' function in higher education." *The American Journal of Sociology* 65(6): 569–76.

—(1960b). *The Open Door College: A Case Study.* New York: McGraw-Hill.

Cofer, J. and Somers, P. (2001). "What Influences Student Persistence At Two-Year Colleges?" *Community College Review* 29(3): 56.

Cohen, A. M. and Brawer, F. B. (2008). *The American Community College,* 5th edn. San Francisco: Jossey-Bass.

College Board Policy and Advocacy Center (2013). "Trends in Higher Education" [website]. Retrieved on June 28, 2013 from: http://trends.collegeboard.org/student-aid/figures-tables/federal-aid#

Commager, H. S. (1950). *The American Mind; an Interpretation of American thought and Character since the 1880's.* New Haven, CT: Yale University Press.

Complete College America (2011). *Time is the Enemy.* Washington, D.C.: Complete College America.

Cooper, W. J. (1928). "The Junior-College Movement in California." *The School Review* 36(6): 409–22.

Cutten, G. (1939). "The Future of the American Liberal-Arts College." *The Journal of Higher Education* 10(2): 59–67.

Day, M. (1981). *Adult Education as a New Educational Frontier: Review of the Journal of Adult Education 1929–1941.* Ann Arbor, MI: University of Michigan.

De los Santos, A. G. and Sutton, F. (2012). "Swirling Students: Articulation Between A Major Community College District and a State-Supported Research University." *Community College Journal of Research & Practice* 36(12): 967–81.

Dewey, J. (2008/1899). "The School and Society," in *The Middle Works of John Dewey, Volume 1, 1899–1901.* Carbondale, IL: Southern Illinois University Press, pp. 3–111.

—(2008/1913). "Should Michigan Have Vocational Education under 'Unit' or 'Dual' Control?" in *The Middle Works of John Dewey, 1899–1924, Volume 7, 1912–1914, Essays Interest and Effort in Education.* Carbondale, IL: Southern Illinois University Press, pp. 85–92.

—(2008/1913). "Some Dangers in the Present Movement for Industrial Education," in *The Middle Works of John Dewey, 1899–1924, Volume 7, 1912–1914, Essays Interest and Effort in Education.* Carbondale, IL: Southern Illinois University Press, pp. 98–103.

—(2008/1913). "Industrial Education and Democracy," in *The Middle Works of John Dewey, 1899–1924, Volume 7, 1912–1914, Essays Interest and Effort in Education.* Carbondale, IL: Southern Illinois University Press, pp. 104–6.

—(2008/1913). "Education from a social perspective," in *The Middle Works of John Dewey, 1899–1924, Volume 7, 1912–1914, Essays Interest and Effort in Education.* Carbondale, IL: Southern Illinois University Press, pp. 113–28.

—(2008/1914). "A Policy of Industrial Education," in *The Middle Works of John Dewey, 1899–1924, Volume 7, 1912–1914, Essays Interest and Effort in Education.* Carbondale, IL: Southern Illinois University Press, pp. 93–8.

—(2008/1915). "Industrial Education—A Wrong Kind," in *The Middle Works of John Dewey, 1899–1924, Volume 8, 1915, Essays, German Philosophy and Politics, Schools of To-morrow*. Carbondale, IL: Southern Illinois University Press, pp. 117–23.

—(2008/1916). "Democracy and Education," in *The Middle Works 1899–1924: John Dewey, Volume 9 Democracy and Education 1916*. Carbondale, IL: Southern Illinois University Press, pp. vii–402.

—(2008/1916). "Universal Service as Education," in *The Middle Works of John Dewey, 1899–1924, Volume 10, 1916–1917, Essays*. Carbondale, IL: Southern Illinois University Press, pp. 183–91.

—(2008/1916). "Force, Violence, and Law," in *The Middle Works of John Dewey, 1899–1924, Volume 10, 1916–1917, Essays*. Carbondale, IL: Southern Illinois University Press, pp. 211–6.

—(2008/1917). "The Modern Trend Toward Vocational Education in Its Effect Upon the Professional and Non-Professional Studies of the University," in *The Middle Works of John Dewey, 1899–1924, Volume 10, 1916–1917, Essays*. Carbondale, IL: Southern Illinois University Press, pp. 151–7.

—(2008/1918). "The Problem of Secondary Education after the War," in *The Later Works of John Dewey, 1925–1953, Volume 17, 1885–1953, Essays*. Carbondale, IL: Southern Illinois University Press, pp. 26–8.

—(2008/1918). "Vocational Education in the Light of the World War," in *The Middle Works of John Dewey, 1899–1924, Volume 11, 1918–1919, Essays*. Carbondale, IL: Southern Illinois University Press, pp. 58–69.

—(2008/1918). "Internal Social Reorganization after the War," in *The Middle Works of John Dewey, 1899–1924, Volume 11, 1918–1919, Essays*. Carbondale, IL: Southern Illinois University Press, pp. 73–86.

—(2008/1920). "Reconstruction in Philosophy," in *The Middle Works of John Dewey, 1899–1924, Volume 12: 1920 Essays, Reconstruction in Philosophy*. Carbondale, IL: Southern Illinois University Press, pp. 79–201.

—(2008/1922). "Human Nature and Conduct," in *The Middle Works of John Dewey, 1899–1924, Volume 14, 1922, Human Nature and Conduct*. Carbondale, IL: Southern Illinois University Press, pp. 4–235.

—(2008/1922). "Public Opinion," in *The Middle Works of John Dewey, 1899–1924, Volume 13, 1922–1922, Essays*. Carbondale, IL: Southern Illinois University Press, pp. 337–44.

—(2008/1922). "Social Purposes in Education," in *The Middle Works of John Dewey, 1899–1924, Volume 15, 1923–1924, Essays*. Carbondale, IL: Southern Illinois University Press, pp. 158–69.

—(2008/1925). "Experience and Nature," in *The Later Works of John Dewey, 1925–1953. Volume 1, 1925, Experience and Nature*. Carbondale, IL: Southern Illinois University Press, pp. 2–327.

—(2008/1925). "Practical Democracy," in *The Later Works of John Dewey, 1925–1953. Volume 2, 1925–1927, Essays, The Public and Its Problems*. Carbondale, IL: Southern Illinois University Press, pp. 213–20.

—(2008/1927). "The Public and its Problems," in *The Later Works of John Dewey, 1925–1953. Volume 2, 1925–1927, Essays, The Public and its Problems*. Carbondale, IL: Southern Illinois University Press, pp. 235–372.

—(2008/1930). "Individualism, Old and New," in *The Later Works of John Dewey, 1925–1953, Volume 5, 1929–1930, Essays, the Sources of a Science Education,*

Individualism, Old and New, and Construction and Criticism. Carbondale, IL: Southern Illinois University Press, pp. 42–124.

—(2008/1931). "American Education Past and Future," in *The Later Works of John Dewey, 1925–1953, Volume 6, 1931–1932, Essays.* Carbondale, IL: Southern Illinois University Press, pp. 90–8.

—(2008/1934). "Education for a Changing Social Order," in *The Later Works of John Dewey, 1925–1953, Volume 9, 1933–1934, Essays, A Common Faith.* Carbondale, IL: Southern Illinois University Press, pp. 158–68.

—(2008/1934). "Education and the Social Order," in *The Later Works of John Dewey, 1925–1953, Volume 9, 1933–1934, Essays, A Common Faith.* Carbondale, IL: Southern Illinois University Press, pp. 175–86.

—(2008/1935). "The Need for Orientation," in *The Later Works of John Dewey, 1925–1953, Volume 11, 1935–1937, Essays, Liberalism and Social Action.* Carbondale, IL: Southern Illinois University Press, pp. 162–6.

—(2008/1935). "Liberalism and Social Action," in J. A. Boydston (ed.), *The Later Works of John Dewey, 1925–1953, Volume 11, 1935–1937, Essays, Liberalism and Social Action.* Carbondale, IL: Southern Illinois University Press, pp. 1–65.

—(2008/1936). "Rationality in Education," in J. A. Boydston (ed.), *The Later Works of John Dewey, 1925–1953, Volume 11, 1935–1937, Essays, Liberalism and Social Action.* Carbondale, IL: Southern Illinois University Press, pp. 391–7.

—(2008/1939). "Freedom and Culture," in J. A. Boydston (ed.), *The Later Works of John Dewey, 1925–1953. Volume 13, 1938–1939, Essays, Experience and Education, Freedom and Culture, and Theory of Valuation.* Carbondale, IL: Southern Illinois University Press, pp. 63–188.

Diggins, J. P. (1994). *The Promise of Pragmatism: Modernism and the Crisis of Knowledge and Authority.* Chicago: University of Chicago Press.

Dougherty, K. J. (1994). *The Contradictory College: The Conflict Origins, Impacts, and Futures of the Community College.* Albany, NY: State University of New York Press.

Dougherty, K. J. and Hong, E. (2006). "Performance accountability as imperfect panacea," in T. Bailey and V. S. Morest (eds), *Defending the Community College Equity Agenda.* Baltimore, MD: Johns Hopkins University Press, pp. 51–86.

Douglass, J. (2000). *The California Idea and American Higher Education: 1850 to the 1960 Master Plan.* Stanford, CA: Stanford University Press.

Du Bois, W. E. B. (1973). *The Correspondence of W. E. B. Du Bois.* Amherst, MA: University of Massachusetts Press.

Duncan, G. J. and Murnane, R. J. (eds) (2011). *Whither Opportunity?: Rising Inequality, Schools, and Children's Life Chances.* New York: Russell Sage Foundation.

Dykhuizen, G. (1973). *The Life and Mind of John Dewey.* Carbondale, IL: Southern Illinois University Press.

Eells, W. C. (1931). *The Junior College.* Boston: Houghton Mifflin Company.

—(1939). "Implications of the Junior College Movement." *The High School Journal* 22(4): 137–44.

Eldridge, M. (2008). *Introduction to the Correspondence of John Dewey, Volume 2: 1919–1939. 4th edn* [Electronic edition.] Charlottesville, VA: InteLelex Corporation.

Elshtain, J. B. (2002). *Jane Addams and the Dream of American Democracy: A Life.* New York: Basic Books.

—(ed.) (2001). *The Jane Addams Reader*. New York: Basic Books.

Ely, M. (ed.) (1948). *Handbook of Adult Education in the United States*. New York: Institute of Adult Education, Teachers College, Columbia University.

Fain, P. (February 13, 2013). "Biting the Bullet on Completion. Inside Higher Ed." Retrieved February 21, 2013, from http://www.insidehighered.com/news/2013/02/20/community-college-learns-boosting-retention-comes-cost

Federal Bureau of Investigation (1943, April 29). *To Whom it May Concern. (16483)*. Charlottesville, VA: InteLelex Corporation.

Fine, B. (1946, January 18). *Big Growth Coming in Junior Colleges, New York Times*, p. 19.

Friedman, T. L. and Mandelbaum, M. (2011). *That Used to be us: How America Fell behind in the World it Invented and How We can Come Back*. New York: Farrar, Straus and Giroux.

Glassman, M., Erdem, G. and Bartholomew, M. (2013). "Action Research and Its History as an Adult Education Movement for Social Change." *Adult Education Quarterly* 63(3): 272–88.

Goldin, C. D. and Katz, L. F. (2009). *The Race between Education and Technology*. Cambridge, MA: Belknap Press of the Harvard University Press.

Goldin, I. (2013). *Divided Nations: Why Global Governance is Failing, and What We can do About it*, 1st edn. New York: Oxford University Press.

Goldrick-Rab, S. (2010). "Challenges and Opportunities for Improving Community College Student Success." *Review of Educational Research* 80(3): 437–69.

Goodwin, C. D. (1995). "The promise of expertise: Walter Lippmann and the policy sciences." *Policy Sciences* 28(4): 317–45.

Gouinlock, J. (1972). *John Dewey's Philosophy of Value*. New York: Humanities Press.

Greller, W. and Drachsler, H. (2012). "Translating Learning into Numbers: A Generic Framework for Learning Analytics." *Journal of Educational Technology & Society* 15(3): 42–57.

Greenleaf, W. J. (1935). "Federal Aid to College Students." *The Journal of Higher Education* 6(2): 94–7.

Grossman, J., Keating, A. D. and Reiff, J. (eds) (2004). *The Encyclopedia of Chicago*. Chicago: University of Chicago Press.

Grubb, W. N. and Lazerson, M. (2004). *The Education Gospel: The Economic Power of Schooling*. Cambridge, MA: Harvard University Press.

Gunn, G. B. (1992). *Thinking across the American Grain: Ideology, Intellect, and the New Pragmatism*. Chicago: University of Chicago Press.

Haggard, W. W. (1930). "An Early Upward Extension of Secondary Education." *The School Review* 38(6): 430–3.

Hanna, J. V. (1930). "Student-Retention in Junior Colleges." *The Journal of Educational Research* 22(1): 1–8.

Hansen, W. L. (1983). "Impact of Student Financial Aid on Access." *Proceedings of the Academy of Political Science* 35(2): 84–96.

Hanushek, E. A., Woessmann, L. and Zhang, L. (2011). *General Education, Vocational Education, and Labor-Market Outcomes over the Life-Cycle* (Working Paper No. 17504). Washington, D.C.: National Bureau of Economic Research.

Harbeson, J. W. (1940). "Meeting the Needs of Terminal Students at the Junior-College Level." *The School Review* 48(8): 577–87.

Harbour, C. P. and Wolgemuth, J. R. (2013). "Giorgio Agamben and the Abandonment Paradigm: A new form of student diversion in public higher education." *The Review of Higher Education* 36(2): 235–54.

Harbour, C. P. and Jaquette, O. (2007). "Advancing an equity agenda at the community college in an age of privatization, performance accountability, and marketization." *Equity & Excellence in Education* 40: 197–207.

Held, D. and McGrew, A. G. (2007). *Globalization Theory: Approaches and Controversies.* Cambridge: Polity.

Hickman, L. A. (2008). *Introduction to the Correspondence of John Dewey, Volume 1: 1871–1918. 4th edn* [Electronic edition.] Charlottesville, VA: InteLelex Corporation.

Honeyman, D. S., Williamson, M. L. and Wattenbarger, J. (1991). *Community College Financing 1990 Challenges for a New Decade.* Washington, D.C.: American Association of Community Colleges.

Hook, S. (1939). *John Dewey, an Intellectual Portrait.* Amherst, NY: Prometheus Books.

Horn, L. and Radwin, D. (2012). *The Completion Arch: Measuring Community College Student Success.* New York: The College Board.

Houle, C. O. (1941). "Adult Education in the Evening Junior College." *The School Review* 49(8): 595–602.

Humphreys, D. (2012). "What's Wrong with the Completion Agenda—And What We Can Do About It?" *Liberal Education* 98(1): 8–17.

Hutchins, R. M. (1933). "The American Educational System." *The School Review* 41(2): 95–100.

—(1948). "The Report of the President's Commission on Higher Education." *Educational Record* 29: 107–22.

Kabat, G. J. (1940). "The People's College." *The Journal of Higher Education* 11(2): 85–9.

Kallen, H. M. (1942). "The War and Education in the United States." *American Journal of Sociology* 48(3): 331–42.

Kane, T. J. and Orszag, P. R. (2003). "Higher education spending: The role of Medicaid and the business cycle," in E. Mintz (ed.), *The Brookings Institution Policy Brief (Policy Brief #124).* Washington, D.C.: The Brookings Institution.

Karabel, J. (1972). "Community colleges and social stratification." *Harvard Educational Review* 41: 521–62.

Katsinas, S. G., Davis, J. E., Friedel, J. N., Koh, J. P. and Grant, P. D. (2013). *The Impact of the New Pell Grant Restrictions on Community Colleges: A Three State Study of Alabama, Arkansas, and Mississippi.* Tuscaloosa, AL: University of Alabama Education Policy Center.

Katz, B. and Bradley, J. (2013). *The Metropolitan Revolution How Cities and Metros are Fixing our Broken Politics and Fragile Economy.* Washington, D.C.: Brookings Institution Press.

Kennedy, D. M. (1999). *Freedom from Fear: The American People in Depression and War, 1929–1945.* New York: Oxford University Press.

—(2009). "What the New Deal Did." *Political Science Quarterly* 124(2): 251–68.

Kharas, H. (2010). *The Emerging Middle Class in Developing Countries.* Paris: OECD Development Centre. Retrieved June 26, 2013 from http://unpan1. un.org/intradoc/groups/public/documents/un-dpadm/unpan044413.pdf

Kisker, C. B. and Ronan, B. (2012). *Civic Engagement in Community Colleges: Mission, Institutionalization, and Future Prospects*. Dayton, OH: Kettering Foundation.

Kotamraju, P. and Blackman, O. (2011). "Meeting the 2020 American Graduation Initiative (AGI) Goal of Increasing Postsecondary Graduation Rates and Completions: A Macro Perspective of Community College Student Educational Attainment." *Community College Journal of Research & Practice* 35(3): 202–19.

Knapp, L. G., Kelly-Reid, J. E. and Ginder, S. A. (2011). *Enrollment in Postsecondary Institutions, Fall 2009; Graduation Rates, 2003 & 2006 Cohorts; and Financial Statistics, Fiscal Year 2009 (NCES 2011-230)*. U.S. Department of Education. Washington, DC: National Center for Education Statistics.

Knight, E. W. (1949). "The Evolving and Expanding Common School." *Annals of the American Academy of Political and Social Science* 265: 92–100.

Knight, L. W. (2005). *Citizen: Jane Addams and the Struggle for Democracy*. Chicago: University of Chicago Press.

—(2010). *Jane Addams: Spirit in Action*. New York: W. W. Norton.

Koos, L. V. (1925). *The Junior-College Movement*. Boston: Ginn and Company.

—(1930). "The junior college." in R. A. Kent (ed.), *Higher Education in America*. Boston: Ginn and Company, pp. 3–33.

Krebs, P., Katsinas, S. G. and Johnson, J. L. (1999). "Illinois community colleges: their history and system." *Community College Journal of Research & Practice* 23(1): 19–41.

Kurtz, P. (2008). "Introduction," in J. A. Boydston (ed.), *The Later Works of John Dewey, 1925–1953, Volume 5: 1919–1930, Essays, The Sources of a Science Education, Individualism, Old and New, and Construction and Criticism*. Carbondale, IL: Southern Illinois University Press, pp. xi– xxxii.

Labaree, D. F. (2010). *Someone Has to Fail: The Zero-Sum Game of Public Schooling*. Cambridge, MA: Harvard University Press.

Letter from M. H. Buckham to D. C. Gilman, April 3, 1883, (00426).

Letter from John Dewey to Alice Chipman Dewey, June 30 and July 2, 1894, (00145).

Letter from John Dewey to Alice Chipman Dewey, Frederick A., and Evelyn Dewey, July 14 and 16, 1894 (00159).

Letter from John Dewey to Alice Chipman Dewey, October 14, 1894, (00209).

Letter from John Dewey to Alice Chipman Dewey, October 19, 1894, (00211).

Letter from John Dewey to Alice Chipman, November 1, 1894, (00218).

Letter from John Dewey to Henry Bawden, November 7, 1911 (02929).

Letter from John Dewey to George Stuart Fullerton, #December 4, 1914 (03265).

Letter from D. C. Gilman to M. H. Buckham, March 30, 1883, (00428)

Levin, J. S. (2001). *Globalizing the Community College: Strategies for Change in the Twenty-first Century*. New York: Palgrave.

Levine, D. O. (1988). *The American College and the Culture of Aspiration, 1915–1940*. Ithaca, NY: Cornell University Press.

Lewis, G. L. (1989). "Trends in student aid: 1963–64 to 1988–89." *Research in Higher Education* 30(6): 547–61.

Lindsey, A. (1942). *The Pullman Strike: The Story of a Unique Experiment and of a Great Labor Upheaval*. Chicago: The University of Chicago Press.

Lippmann, W. (1914). *Drift and Mastery; an Attempt to Diagnose the Current Unrest*. New York: M. Kennerley.

—(1922). *Public Opinion*. New York: Harcourt, Brace and Company.

—(1925). *The Phantom Public*. New York: Harcourt, Brace, and Company.

Long, B. T. and Riley, E. (2007). "Financial Aid: A Broken Bridge to College Access?" *Harvard Educational Review* 77(1): 39–63.

Loss, C. P. (2012). *Between Citizens and the State: The Politics of American Higher Education in the 20th Century*. Princeton, NJ: Princeton University Press.

Luskin, J. (1972). *Lippmann, Liberty, and the Press*. Tuscaloosa, AL: University of Alabama Press.

McCormick, A. C. (2003). "Swirling and Double-Dipping: New Patterns of Student Attendance and Their Implications for Higher Education," in J. E. King, E. L. Anderson and M. E. Corrigan (eds), *Changing Student Attendance Patterns: Challenges for Policy and Practice. New Directions for Higher Education*, No. 121. San Francisco: Jossey – Bass, pp. 13–24.

McDowell, F. M. (1919). *The Junior College*. Washington, D.C.: Bureau of Education, Department of the Interior.

Maddox, C. R. (1934). "Functional Changes in Original Structure." *Review of Educational Research* 4(4): 375–81.

Mahbubani, K. (2013). *The Great Convergence: Asia, the West, and the Logic of one World*. New York: Public Affairs.

Marcus, J. (July 11, 2011). "Two years after Obama's college graduation initiative, major obstacles remain." Hechinger Report. Retrieved June 13, 2013, from http://hechingerreport.org/content/two-years-after-obamas-college-graduation-initiative-major-obstacles-remain_5946/

Marres, N. (2013). "Why political ontology must be experimentalized: On eco-show homes as devices of participation." *Social Studies of Science* 43(3): 417–43.

Martin, A. and Lehren, A. W. (May 13, 2012). A Generation Hobbled by College Debt, *New York Times*, pp. A.1, A20–21.

Matthews, C. M. (October 18, 2012). *Federal Support for Academic Research*. Washington, D.C.: Congressional Research Service.

Mayer, M. S. (1957). *Young Man in a Hurry: The Story of William Rainey Harper, first President of the University of Chicago*. Chicago: The University of Chicago Alumni Association.

Medicare Prescription Drug, Improvement, and Modernization Act of 2003. Public Law 108–173, 117 Stat. 2066 (2003).

Meier, K. M. (2008). *The Community College Mission: History and Theory, 1930–2000*. Tucson, AZ: The University of Arizona.

Menand, L. (2001). *The Metaphysical Club*. New York: Farrar, Straus, and Giroux.

Miller, D. L. (1996). *City of the Century: The Epic of Chicago and the Making of America*. New York: Simon & Schuster.

Mishel, L., Bivens, J., Gould, E. and Shierholz, H. (2012). *The State of Working America*. Ithaca, NY: ILR Press.

Morrison, R. H. (1935). Emergency junior colleges in New Jersey: A study of their need, nature, instruction staff, student body, management, and accomplishment. State of New Jersey Emergency Relief Administration.

Murnane, R. J. (2013). U.S High School Graduation Rates: Patterns and Explanations (Working Paper No. 18701). National Bureau of Economic Research. Retrieved from http://www.nber.org/papers/w18701

Naegele, T. (1983). "The Guaranteed Student Loan Program: Do Lenders' Risks Exceed Their Rewards." *Hastings Law Journal* 34: 599–633.

New, M. J. (2010). "U.S. State Tax and Expenditure Limitations: A Comparative Political Analysis." *State Politics & Policy Quarterly* 10(1): 25–50.

Newman, F., Couturier, L. and Scurry, J. (2004). *The Future of Higher Education: Rhetoric, Reality, and the Risks of the Market.* San Francisco: Jossey-Bass Publishers.

New York Times (June 27, 1894). "Pullman car strike begun: Indications that it will cause great trouble," *New York Times*, p. 8.

—(July 1, 1894). "Greatest strike in history: Pullman boycott will involve scores of industries," *New York Times*, p. 1.

O'Banion, T. (1997). *A Learning College for the 21st Century.* Lanham, MD: Rowman & Littlefield Publishers.

O'Donnell, M. E. (May 8, 1910). "Suffragettes of yesterday and today," *Chicago Daily Tribune*, p. F1.

Obama, B. O. (July 14, 2009). President's Remarks at Macomb Community College, Warren Michigan.

OECD. (2012). *Education at a Glance—OECD Indicators 2012—Country Note—United States.* Paris: OECD.

Oliff, P., Palacios, V., Johnson, I. and Leachman, M. (March 19, 2013). "Recent Deep State Higher Education Cuts May Harm Students and the Economy for Years to Come." Center on Budget and Policy Priorities. Retrieved June 26, 2013 from http://www.cbpp.org/files/3-19-13sfp.pdf

Orfield, G. (1990). "Public Policy and College Opportunity." *American Journal of Education* 98(4): 317–50.

Outland, G. E. (1937). "Curriculum Planning in an Emergency Junior College." *Educational Administration and Supervision* 23: 143–8.

Palmer, J. (2013). "State Fiscal Support for Community Colleges," in J. S. Levin and S. T. Kater (eds), *Understanding Community Colleges.* New York: Routledge, pp. 171–83.

Papke, D. R. (1999). *Pullman Case.* Lawrence, KS: University Press of Kansas.

Patterson, J. T. (1997). *Grand Expectations: The United States, 1945–1974.* New York: Oxford University Press.

Paxton, R. O. and Hessler, J. (2011). *Europe in the Twentieth Century,* 5th edn. New York: Wadsworth Publishing.

Pedersen, R. P. (2000). *The Origins and Development of the early Public Junior College: 1900–1940.* New York: Columbia University.

Piketty, T. (2014). *Capital in the Twenty-first Century.* Cambridge, MA: The Belknap Press of Harvard University Press.

Piketty, T. and Saez, E. (2013). "Top Incomes and the Great Recession: Recent Evolutions and Policy Implications." *IMF Economic Review* 61(3): 456–78.

Posner, R. A. (2009). *A Failure of Capitalism: The Crisis of '08 and the Descent into Depression.* Cambridge, MA: Harvard University Press.

—(2010). *The Crisis of Capitalist Democracy.* Cambridge, MA: Harvard University Press.

President's Commission on Higher Education. (1947). *Higher Education for American Democracy, A Report* (Volumes I – VI). Washington, D.C.: U.S. Government Printing Office.

Putnam, R. D. (2000). *Bowling Alone: The Collapse and Revival of American Community*. New York: Simon & Schuster.

Rainey, H. P. (1930). "The Future of the Arts College." *The Journal of Higher Education* 1(7): 381–6.

Ratner, S. (2008). "Introduction," in J. A. Boydston (ed.), *The Later Works of John Dewey, 1925–1953, Volume 6: 1931–1932, Essays*. Carbondale, IL: Southern Illinois University Press, pp. xi–xxiii.

Ravitch, D. (2013). *Reign of Error: The Hoax of the Privatization Movement and the Danger to America's Public Schools*. New York: Alfred A. Knopf.

Reardon, S. F. (2011). "The Widening Academic Achievement Gap Between the Rich and the Poor: New Evidence and Possible Explanations," in G. J. Duncan and R. J. Murnane (eds), *Whither Opportunity? Rising Inequality, Schools, and Children's Life Chances*. New York: Russell Sage Foundation, pp. 91–115.

Reavis, W. C. (1935). "Federal Participation in Public Education in Illinois in 1933–34." *The Elementary School Journal* 35(5): 349–58.

Reich, R. B. (2010). *Aftershock: The Next Economy and America's Future*. New York: Alfred A. Knopf.

Reid, A. E. (1966). *A History of the California Public Junior College Movement*. Los Angeles, CA: University of Southern California.

Rhoades, G. (2012). "The Incomplete Completion Agenda." *Liberal Education* 98(1): 18–25.

Robinson, K. (2011). *Out of Our Minds: Learning to be Creative*. Oxford: Capstone.

Rodrik, D. (2012). *The Globalization Paradox: Democracy and the Future of the World Economy*. New York: W. W. Norton & Company.

Roherty, B. M. (1997). "The Price of Passive Resistance in Financing Higher Education," in P. M. Callan and J. E. Finney (eds), *Public and Private Financing of Higher Education*. Phoenix, AZ: American Council on Education, pp. 3–29.

Rockefeller, S. C. (1991). *John Dewey: Religious Faith and Democratic Humanism*. New York: Columbia University Press.

Rorty, R. (1979). *Philosophy and the Mirror of Nature*. Princeton, NJ: Princeton University Press.

—(1982). *Consequences of Pragmatism: Essays, 1972–1980*. Minneapolis: University of Minnesota Press.

Rosa, H. (2013). *Social Acceleration: A New Theory of Modernity*. New York: Columbia University Press.

Ross, R. (2008). "Introduction," in J. A. Boydston (ed.), *The Middle Works of John Dewey, 1899–1924, Volume 12: 1920 Essays, Reconstruction in Philosophy*. Carbondale, IL: Southern Illinois University Press, pp. ix– xxx.

Rowden, D. (ed.) (1934). *Handbook of Adult Education in the United States*. New York: American Association for Adult Education.

—(1936). *Handbook of Adult Education in the United States*. New York: American Association for Adult Education.

Ryan, A. (1995). *John Dewey and the High Tide of American Liberalism*. New York: W. W. Norton.

Salvatore, N. (1982). *Eugene V. Debs: Citizen and Socialist*. Champaign, IL: University of Illinois Press.

Sassen, S. (2007). *A Sociology of Globalization*. New York: W. W. Norton.

Scahill, J. (2013). *Dirty Wars: The World is a Battlefield*. New York: Nation Books.

Schlesinger, A. M. (1987). *The Coming of the New Deal*. Norwalk, CT: Easton Press.

Science (April 29, 1910). "Scientific notes and news." *Science* 32(800): 662.

Shear, M. D. and de Vise, D. (July 15, 2009). "Obama Announces Community College Plan; $12 Billion Will Fund New Web Courses, Construction and Innovation Grants," *The Washington Post*, p. A.2. Washington, D.C., United States.

Shiller, R. J. (2012). *Finance and the Good Society*. Princeton, NJ: Princeton University Press.

Simpson, M. W. (2007). "National Emergency and Federal Junior Colleges in New Jersey." *American Educational History Journal* 34(1/2): 173–87.

Smith, H. (2012). *Who Stole the American Dream?* New York: Random House.

Snyder, T. D. (1993). *120 Years of American Education: A Statistical Portrait*. U.S. Department of Education. Washington, DC: National Center for Education Statistics.

Snyder, T. D. and Dillow, S. A. (2011). *Digest of Education Statistics 2010*. Washington, D.C.: U.S. Department of Education. Washington, DC: National Center for Education Statistics.

Steel, R. (1980). *Walter Lippmann and the American Century*. Boston: Little, Brown.

Stevenson, C. L. (2008). "Introduction," in J. A. Boydston (ed.), *The Middle Works of John Dewey, 1899–1924, Volume 5: 1908 Ethics*. Carbondale, IL: Southern Illinois University Press, pp. lx–xxxiv.

Stiglitz, J. E. (2012). *The Price of Inequality*. New York: W. W. Norton & Co.

Storr, R. J. (1966). *Harper's University, the Beginnings: A History of the University of Chicago*. Chicago: University of Chicago Press.

Stubblefield, H. W. (1994). *Adult Education in the American Experience: From the Colonial Period to the Present*. San Francisco: Jossey-Bass Publishers.

Taylor, P. & Pew Research Center (2014), *The Next America: Boomers, Millennials, and the Looming Generational Showdown*. New York: Public Affairs.

The Grapevine (2013). "State Fiscal Support for Higher Education, by State, Fiscal Years 2007–08 (FY08), 2010–11 (FY11), 2011–12 (FY12), 2012–13 (FY13)." Normal, IL: Illinois State University. Retrieved July 14, 2013 from: http://grapevine.illinoisstate.edu/tables/FY13/Table1_FY13.pdf

Thomas, D. and Seely-Brown, J. (2011). *A New Culture of Learning: Cultivating the Imagination for a World of Constant Change*. Lexington, KY.: CreateSpace.

Time (1933, September 18). "Schools at the Turn." *Time* 22(12): 22.

Time (1934, May 28). "Studebaker for Zook." *Time* 23(22): 52.

Time (1942, October 26). "Who will Run the Colleges?" *Time* 40(17): 83.

Time (1955, May 15). "No Job for Mollycoddles." *Time* 55(20): 66.

United States Treasury (January 16, 2013). "Historical Debt Outstanding: Annual 2000–2012." Retrieved June 26, 2013, from http://www.treasurydirect.gov/govt/reports/pd/histdebt/histdebt_histo5.htm

United States Census Bureau (1961). *Eighteenth Census of the United States*. Washington, D.C.: Department of Commerce.

United States Census Office (1901). *Twelfth Census of the United States, Taken in the Year 1900*. Washington, D.C.: Department of the Interior.

United States Treasury Department (November 30, 2013). *Monthly Statement of the Public Debt of the United States, November 30, 2013*. Washington, D.C.: The Bureau of the Fiscal Service.

Vangiezen, R. and Schwenk, A. E. (2001). "Compensation from before World War I through the Great Depression." *Compensation and Working Conditions* 6(3): 17–22.

Vaughan, G. B. (1985). "Maintaining open access and comprehensiveness," in D. Puyear (ed.), *Maintaining Institutional Integrity. New Directions for Community Colleges*, No. 52. San Francisco: Jossey-Bass, pp. 17–28.

—(2006). *The Community College Story*. Washington, D.C.: American Association of Community Colleges.

Walters, G. (2012). "It's Not So Easy: The Completion Agenda and the States." *Liberal Education* 98(1): 34–9.

Wartime Activities (1942a, September). *Junior College Journal* 13(1): 33–9.

—(1942b, October). *Junior College Journal* 13(2): 100–4.

—(1943, February). *Junior College Journal* 13(6): 303.

Weerts, D. J. and Ronca, J. M. (2012). "Understanding Differences in State Support for Higher Education Across States, Sectors, and Institutions: A Longitudinal Study." *Journal of Higher Education* 83(2): 155–85.

Westbrook, R. B. (1992). "Schools for industrial democrats: The social origins of John Dewey's philosophy of education." *American Journal of Education* 100(4): 401–19.

—(1993). *John Dewey and American Democracy*. Ithaca, NY: Cornell University Press.

Wiebe, R. H. (1966). *The Search for Order, 1877–1920*. New York: Hill and Wang.

Willey, M. W. (1937). *Depression, Recovery and Higher Education*. New York: McGraw-Hill.

Wirth, A. G. (1966). *John Dewey as Educator; Design for Work in Education, 1894–1904*. New York: Wiley.

Wolin, S. S. (2004). *Politics and Vision: Continuity and Innovation in Western Political Thought*. Princeton, N.J.: Princeton University Press.

Young, R. J. (1950). *An Analysis and Evaluation of General Legislation Pertaining to Public Junior Colleges*. Boulder, CO: University of Colorado.

Zimmerman, J. G. (1978). *College Culture in the Midwest: 1890–1930*. Charlottesville, VA: University of Virginia.

Zook, G. F. (1922). "The junior college." *The School Review* 30(8): 574–83.

—(1926). "The Junior College Movement." *School and Society* 23(594): 601–5.

—(1929). "Is the Junior College a Menace or a Boon?" *The School Review* 37(6): 415–25.

—(1934). "Uncle Sam Faces a Crisis in Education." *Congressional Digest* 13(2): 40–64.

—(1943). "Fifteen Months of Negotiations." *Journal of Educational Sociology* 16(9): 562–76.

Index

Addams, Jane   48
adult education movement   74–6
American Association for Adult
    Education   75
    Journal of Adult Education   75
American Association of Community
    Colleges (AACC)   1, 4, 13, 30,
    100, 105, 109
    *Building Communities: A Vision
    for a New Century* (1988)   100,
    101, 105, 106, 107, 110, 112,
    113, 117,
    *Reclaiming the American Dream:
    Community Colleges and the
    Nation's Future* (2012)   4, 5,
    26, 30, 101, 109, 110, 111,
    113, 117
American Association of Junior
    Colleges (AAJC)   90
American Association of Teachers
    Colleges   144, 145
American Civil War   12, 44, 45
American Council on Education
    67, 81
American Graduation Initiative   1, 2
Armour Institute of Technology   47
Art Institute of Chicago   48
Asia-Pacific region   37

Big Data   34
Boggs, George   1
Boydston, Jo Ann   vii
Brint, Steven   13, 27, 100, 103, 104,
    105, 111,
Brookwood Labor College   141
Brown, J. Stanley   61, 62
Brown, Pat   95
Buckham, Matthew   45
Bureau of the Census   90
Burlington, Vermont   44

California   13, 17, 20, 59, 63, 65,
    93, 94, 95, 96, 98
    California Community College
        System   87, 96
    California State University
        System   87, 94, 95, 96
    General Assembly   64
    Master Plan   87, 94, 95, 96, 98
    University of California
        System   94, 95, 96
Carnegie Foundation   75
Center on Budget and Policy
    Priorities   40
Chamber of Commerce   22
Chicago, Illinois   11, 12, 46, 47, 48,
    49, 59, 60, 62, 118
China   37, 88, 130
The Civil Rights Act of 1964   97,
    112, 153
Clark, Burton   13, 27, 64, 100, 102,
    103, 104, 105, 111
Cleveland, Grover   47
Columbia University   44, 49, 50, 141
Complete College America   3, 6
Completion Agenda   3, 4, 5, 6, 8, 12,
    14, 17, 26, 27, 32, 42, 110, 111, 152
conventional history, the   29–31

Debs, Eugene   46, 47
Dennett, Tyler   145, 146
Dewey, Alice (formerly Alice
    Chipman)   45, 47, 48, 132
Dewey, Evelyn   47
Dewey, Frederick   47
Dewey, Gordon   49
Dewey, John   vi, vii, viii, 7, 8, 10, 11,
    12, 14, 23, 28, 34, 43, 44–55,
    117–26, 127–40, 141–51, 152–9
    *American Education Past and
    Future*   142

Democracy and Education   7, 14, 50, 54, 117–26, 127, 136, 140, 155, 156
Education and the Social Order   54
Education for a Changing Social Order   142, 144, 145, 146
Education from a Social Perspective   51, 52, 53, 156
Ethics   49, 50
Freedom and Culture   142, 148, 150, 151, 159
Great Community   127–40, 142, 144, 147, 148, 157
Great Society   127–40
How We Think   50
Human Nature and Conduct   14, 130, 131, 155
Individualism, Old and New   142–4
Industrial Education and Democracy   51
Industrial Education—A Wrong Kind   51
Laboratory School, University of Chicago   49
Liberalism and Social Action   142, 148, 149, 150
The Need for Orientation   142, 146
occupations   124, 125, 129, 157
A Policy of Industrial Education   51
Practical Democracy   135
The Problem of Secondary Education   130
The Public and Its Problems   14, 135–40, 141, 151, 157, 158
Rationality in Education   54
Reconstruction in Philosophy   130
The School and Society   47, 49
Should Michigan Have Vocational Education under 'Unit' or 'Dual' Control?   51
Some Dangers in the Present Movement for Industrial Education   51
Universal Service as Education   129
Vocational Education in the Light of the World War   128, 129
Dewey, Morris   49
Donahoe Act   95
Draper, Andrew   61, 62

Eells, Walter   61, 63, 64, 70, 71, 72, 74, 83
The Junior College   70
emergency junior colleges   13, 74, 80, 81, 85, 153
Engineering, Science, and Management War Training Program   88
English as a Second Language   22

Federal Bureau of Investigation   53
Federal Emergency Relief Act of 1933   79
Financial Crisis of 2007–08   3, 30, 40, 41, 101, 108, 109, 112, 152, 153
Folwell, William Watts   65
Fresno High School (California)   63

generational equity   12, 32, 38, 39, 42, 152
Gilman, Daniel   45
globalization   12, 32, 35, 36, 37, 38, 42
Goldman, Emma   141
Great Depression   8, 13, 14, 34, 41, 74, 76, 77, 78, 79, 80–3, 85, 86, 140, 141–51, 153, 158
Great Recession of 2007–09   3, 30, 40, 41, 101, 108, 109, 112, 152, 153

Harper, William Raney   45, 46, 49, 60, 61
Heidegger, Martin   54
Hickman, Larry   45, 50
Higher Education Act of 1965   87, 97, 108, 112, 153
Higher Education Facilities Act of 1963   87
Hochwalt, Frederick   92
Hoover, Herbert   141
Houle, Cyril   83, 84
Hull House   48
Hutchins, Robert   78, 79, 80, 92,

Illinois   59, 62, 63, 65, 72
income inequality   4, 5, 6, 12, 26, 27, 32, 33, 34, 36, 42, 60, 101, 111, 112, 152
information and communications technologies (ICT)   34, 35
institutional mission   9, 23

Japan 33, 130
Johns Hopkins University 45, 49
Johnson, Lyndon B. 97
Joliet, Illinois 59, 60, 61, 62
Jordan, David Starr 50, 63
junior college 8, 11, 12, 13, 28, 29,
    47, 74–99, 102, 103, 104, 111,
    130, 153, 159,
junior college movement 59–73

Kaiser Wilhelm II 118
Karabel, Jerome 13, 27, 100, 103,
    104, 105, 111
Kennedy, John 97
Kenyon College 135
Koos, Leonard 68, 69, 70, 72,
    74, 80
    The Junior College Movement 69

Lange, Alexis 63
League for Independent Political
    Action (LIPA) 142
League for Industrial Democracy 141
leaning analytics 12, 32, 34, 35,
    42, 152
Lenin, Vladimir 147
Lehren, Martin 39
Lippmann, Walter 14, 131, 132–5
    The Phantom Public 134, 135
    Public Opinion 132–4
Loss, Christopher 98
McCarthy, Joseph 53
McDowell, Floyd Marion 65, 66, 68,
    69, 70, 72
McGuire, Martin R. P. 92
Macomb Community College 1
Martin, Andrew 39
Massive Open Online Courses
    (MOOCs) 34
Medicaid 24, 25, 108, 112
Medicare 38, 136
Menand, Louis 44
Modesto Junior College 64

Nagasaki, Japan 53
The Nation 141
National Academy of Sciences 50
National Defense Education Act
    of 1958 (NDEA) 96, 97
National Park College 89

Nazi regime 88, 93, 147, 148
New Haven YMCA 89
New Jersey 80, 81
New Republic 128, 132, 134,
    135, 142,
New York 12, 49, 50, 75, 94, 128,
    132, 141
New York Times 39, 46
normal schools 65–7, 72, 153
normative vision 7–14, 23, 28, 55, 59,
    87–99, 100–13, 117, 149, 152–9

Obama, Barack 1, 2
O'Banion, Terry 34
Oil City, Pennsylvania 45
open door admissions policy 21

Patient Protection and Affordable
    Care Act (Obamacare) 2
Pearl Harbor 88, 89
Pell Grant Program 97, 109
People's Lobby 141
Pew Research Center 38
Plato 118
post-baccalaureate reverse transfers
    (PBRTs) 20
President's Commission on Civil
    Rights 93
Presidents Commission on Higher
    Education (The Truman
    Commission) 13, 67, 82, 87,
    91, 92, 93, 98, 111, 113, 152
private liberal arts college 65–7,
    74, 76, 85, 153
public higher education funding 12,
    32, 40–2, 152
Pullman Strike 46, 47, 118
Putnam, Robert 107

Rainey, Homer 76, 77
Rhode Island 17
Robin Moor 88
Rockefeller, John 45
Roosevelt, Franklin 67, 79, 85, 90,
    141, 147
Rorty, Richard 11, 54

San Francisco Junior College 89
San Jose Junior College 102, 103
Science and Technology Studies 11

Servicemen's Readjustment Act of
    1944 (GI Bill of Rights)   13, 87,
    90, 91, 93, 98, 111, 153
Sinclair, Upton   48, 60
    The Jungle   48, 60
Social Security   38
Soviet Union   14, 88, 91, 147, 148
Spencer, Herbert   118
Stalin, Joseph   147
Stanford University   50, 63, 70, 79
Starr, Ellen Gates   48
Student Aid and Fiscal Responsibility
    Act of 2009   1
student loan crisis   39

Tappan, Henry   65
tax and expenditure limitations
    (TELs)   24, 108, 112
Taylor, Paul   38
technological change   12, 32, 34,
    42, 152
Time magazine   89
Truman, Harry   67, 82, 91
Tufts, James   50
Twain, Mark   7

United States Census Office   60, 94
United State Treasury Department   3, 41
United Way   22
University of Akron   67
University of California, Berkeley
    50, 63, 78
University of California,
    Los Angeles   141

University of Chicago   11, 44, 45,
    47, 49, 60, 62, 78, 79
University of Illinois   49, 61
University of Johannesburg   141
University of Michigan   45
University of Minnesota   45
University of Paris   141
University of St Andrews   141
University of Vermont   45
University of Virginia   148
US Army   63, 88, 89
US Navy   63, 88, 89

Vermont   44, 45

Walter Reed Hospital   89
War Against Terror   3
Warren, Michigan   1
Washington Post   1, 2
Wellesley College   88
Westbrook, Robert   11
Williams College   145
Wittgenstein, Ludwig   54
Wolin, Sheldon   11
women's suffrage   50
World War I   14, 118, 128, 129,
    133, 139
World War II   8, 12, 13, 29, 75,
    84, 87, 88, 90, 91, 93, 96,
    98, 107, 153
Wyoming   20

Zook, George   67, 68, 70, 72, 74,
    81, 82, 83, 85, 90